Catherine Spencer is a former captain of the England women's rugby team. She has written for mainstream and rugby media and worked as a studio pundit and commentator for the BBC, ITV and Sky Sports. She was named England Player of the Year in 2006 and received a Rugby Union Writers' Club Special Award in 2011. She is the founder of the speaker agency Inspiring Women and Patron of the charity Tag Rugby Trust.

MUD, MAUL, MASCARA

CATHERINE SPENCER

unbound

First published in 2020
This paperback edition first published in 2021

Unbound
Level 1, Devonshire House, One Mayfair Place, London W1J 8AJ
www.unbound.com

Text Design by PDQ Digital Media Solutions Ltd.

A CIP record for this book is available from the British Library

ISBN 978-1-80018-085-7 (paperback)
ISBN 978-1-78352-813-4 (hardback)
ISBN 978-1-78352-814-1 (ebook)

Printed in Great Britain by Clays Ltd, Elcograf S.p.A

1 3 5 7 9 8 6 4 2

This book is for my family – to my parents, Nigel and Jane, and to my brothers, Martin and Gregory. Giving you the 'nod'. Thank you for your support, encouragement, pride and love.

To my husband, Jeremy, you have been with me in the aftermath of my rugby journey. You have seen me at my lowest but you have now helped me to look forward. My life has changed so much since I met you. I have so much to thank you for. I love you; today, tomorrow, forever.

To Stephen Jones (of rugby journalism fame), for telling me repeatedly that I *have* to write this book. Your words spurred me on. Thank you.

This book is also for me. I needed this book, more than I realised when I started it.

Contents

Introduction

Never Getting My Enough

When we talk about our 'life' what do we really mean? How do we define ourselves? How do other people define us? Through our work, our gender, our age, where we live? For years I described my life as playing rugby for England. I defined my life by the all-encompassing drive to win a World Cup. I was Catherine Spencer the rugby player. Rugby was not my only job however; I did not get paid to play rugby, so I went to work because I had to, in order to pay the bills, but when I walked out of the office or turned my laptop off, my personal and emotional life was completely devoted to playing rugby for England. That was my reason for being, this was me, my focus. On 5 September 2010, on the morning of the World Cup final, the *Independent on Sunday* ran an article. When asked what we would gain if we won the World Cup my reply was: 'Just the glory of holding the World Cup; that's enough.' That's all it was about for me; that is what everything was about. But I never got my enough.

In August 2014 I was working as a studio pundit for Sky Sports, watching the England women's rugby team win the World Cup. I watched with envy as the captain Katy Mclean lifted the World Cup trophy aloft, I watched with immense agony as former team mates and friends showed such joy on their faces. I knew the extremity of their emotions because at that exact same moment I too had tears streaming down my face. But my tears were shed for the hurt that I had felt four years previously and will always continue to feel; just as extreme as their elation, but a universe of emotions away. A wound that had started to heal over four long years was now destructively torn open in just a few short minutes whilst watching England Women finally win and lift the coveted World Cup.

In 2006 I had to stand with my team mates at the end of the World Cup final watching New Zealand celebrate their win after a game that we could have won; in 2010 I had to watch my opposing captain, Melissa Ruscoe of New Zealand take to the podium and lift the trophy after we lost by 3 points in a game that we should have won. In 2014 I watched England Women win a World Cup final after I retired. I felt bitterness, jealousy, pain and massive hurt. If England had not won in 2014, my own 2006 and 2010 World Cup final wounds would be two scars I would feel proud of; now I am ashamed of them. Now that England Women have won the World Cup after my time I feel that my battle scars are worth nothing. Because what do you really win for coming second? How do I get over this? How do I find purpose and direction in my life that makes my battle scars worth the pain? Do I cover them up? Do I take a new path, or do I use my pain to fuel what comes next?

In 2017 I was on media duty once more, this time on commentary. I witnessed England lose to New Zealand in the final, in front of a packed stadium; and because of that my road to recovery, my transition through retirement, may just have had the kick-start it needed. My own World Cup final losses to New Zealand were pretty good in comparison. Weren't they? Someone pointed out to me recently that I am the England captain who has led her team closer to victory than any other against New Zealand in a World Cup final. Does this mean that it is possible to start to feel proud of my war wounds again? Can this really happen? At the final whistle in 2017 I took a moment to try to understand my emotions but I couldn't feel any. I wanted to but I couldn't. I was numb. I was devoid. My hope? That in 2021 my emotions will return, that I will either feel hurt for England not winning or immense joy watching them lift the trophy. Time will tell on both fronts. At that game in 2017 some of my former team mates, who had retired later than me and had played in the 2014 victory, really struggled to watch England lose; their emotion was clear to see. I, on the other hand, felt no emotion. If anything, and as hard it is to write this, I was pleased that England did not beat New Zealand in that final.

People say that England Women finally won in 2014 because of those that fought before them, those that paved the way for others to follow and aspire to, those that laid foundations upon which others would find glory. Those who build such foundations for others, the worker ants, these are selfless people. I was one of those who went before, but I was not selfless, I was selfish; I wanted to win a World Cup. It was my dream. I did not devote my life to building foundations for others; I devoted my life to achieving my dream. I made choices to miss best friends' weddings (Caroline, I will forever be gutted that I missed your amazing day), I made a personal choice to not develop a career, I made choices to hardly see friends, I made the choice to not spend quality time with my boyfriend, I made the choice to justify this dream. I didn't do this to allow those younger than me to achieve my dream instead of me. I did it for me. All for me.

I had learned to feel proud of my rugby 'career' and for several years I really have enjoyed telling my story, but this has been a huge challenge since 17 August 2014 when the World Cup trophy was held high by an England arm. Retirement is tough, making your own decision to stop doing the thing that you love is tough, relinquishing any chance of achieving your dream is tough, watching other people achieve your dream without you three years on is indescribably tough. There is no life manual for this, no self-help book, no instruction pamphlet to turn to.

After the 2014 World Cup final, once filming finished in the studio, I was taken back home to my house in Kent by taxi. I let myself in, made myself a bowl of pasta and a large cup of tea and just sat in the dark. I hardly ate, I felt as though I had just broken up from a relationship; slightly ill, shattered, sad but also very aware that some of my closest friends were on the other side of the English Channel, enjoying what was probably the best night of their lives, celebrating the fulfilment of their dreams. This was to date the biggest night ever for women's rugby, something that I felt immensely passionate about; why could I not feel happy? I was enduring one of the worst nights of my life, on my own. Sitting in my own home, a place of such familiarity, but feeling so incredibly lost. In that night, more than any other night, I didn't know who I was. Every way I used to define myself was now taunting me, haunting me. Catherine Spencer, former England captain, and failure.

Chapter One
The Lost Dream

I have a photo taken at the end of the 2006 World Cup final (17 September) of the forward pack along with our forwards coach, Graham Smith. You can see the tears in my eyes as I crouched down at the front of the photo alongside Helen 'Rob' Clayton. You can see the absolute dejection and misery on my face. I now know that the pain I felt then was nothing compared to what I would feel four years later, or even eight years on in retirement. If I knew then what the future was going to hold, would I have changed my path? How would I have coped if I had known what was to come. I always say that we could have won but the Black Ferns were without doubt the best team on the pitch that day. I remember thinking that I had never ever had to work so hard at every single breakdown as I did in that game. It was energy-sapping. It was the hardest match that I had ever played in.

I don't remember much about the detail of the game other than the overall feeling of it all. I remember it was cold, really cold – playing in Edmonton, Alberta, we experienced extremes of weather. During the pool games the challenge was dealing with the heat, but the temperature dropped significantly the night before the final and the supporters (what there were of them) were wrapped in blankets, trying to keep warm. As a squad we were hugely confident before the game. During our walk and stretch the morning of the match I was walking alongside Rob, who was on the bench after Maggie beat her to the 7 shirt. Rob was someone I looked up to and I was lucky enough to receive my England rose from her at my first call-up in 2004. She epitomised everything that any of us should have been about: complete devotion to the cause, the cause that was the England team. When Maggie started to take over from Rob to become the first choice 7, it must have been hard for Rob, but she mentored Maggie, she taught her what she knew, she invested in the future to the detriment of her own selection. We were talking on that morning of the final, saying that we knew we were going to win. I was not just saying it – I thought it, I knew it. But we didn't.

In 2006 I was a relative newbie in the squad; I had won my first cap just two and a half years before and this was my first experience of a Women's World Cup. I did not watch the 2002 World Cup that was held in Spain when some of my friends had travelled over to support one of our club team mates who was representing Japan, and I do not remember any media coverage or access to the tournament from the UK. 2006 was a brand-new experience. I remember my England coach, Geoff Richards, phoning me up to tell me that I was in the squad. I was already feeling fairly confident that I would get a seat on the plane – I had worn the number 8 shirt in nearly every game since the 2004 Six Nations and I had won England Player of the Year following the 2006

Six Nations just a few months earlier, but hearing those words on the phone, 'Congratulations, you are selected as part of the twenty-six-player squad to travel to Canada' – was really special. I had made my first big step up in my international career. I was going to represent England at a World Cup. Our aim back then was to go and win. Why would we aim for anything less?

Everyone was talking about an England v New Zealand final even before the tournament started. That was pressure for us, but I am sure that other teams involved were angry that they had swiftly been cast aside in any external expectations. We played our group games against the USA, South Africa and France. The USA were a tough, physical team to play against, as you might imagine. Athletic, strong and determined but with less rugby pedigree than England, less depth of knowledge, not so streetwise. We won the game 18-nil and went on to play what would be a much easier game against South Africa, a relatively young nation in women's rugby terms. In 2005 we played against them in England when they travelled over to tour and beat them 101-nil, with yours truly scoring a hat-trick. We knew that we would win our pool game against them – that was not arrogance but justified confidence. I was to be rested completely in that game and watched from the side-lines – craving to be on the pitch in a more open game. The score was 74 points to 8. Following that we played France in our last pool game. To put this fixture in context, they had been the best team in Europe for several years until we beat them in the 2006 Six Nations just a few months earlier. In 2004 we lost away to them on my second cap and first start and the following year we lost to them again, this time at home. Our Six Nations victory in 2006 still remains one of my favourite games ever and set us in good stead leading into the 2006 World Cup.

My most vivid memory from the pool games section of the tournament was not on the playing pitch, however, but rather saying goodbye to my twin brother Gregory after our game against France. He had come out to Canada to support me but had to fly home early to start a PGCE course. His university would not let him defer his start by just a few days so that he could watch his twin sister represent her country in a World Cup. I have a feeling that if he had been a sibling of a member of the men's 2003 World Cup squad the university would have bent over backwards to accommodate a later start, but that was how it was. At the end of the France game in the changing room everyone was feeling pretty chuffed after we beat them 27-8. Job well done and into the semi-finals – but I was an emotional wreck. I spoke to Gregory on the pitch at the end of the game, knowing that he was heading directly to the airport, and we gave each other a hug. Me trying not to cry, him trying not to cry. The bubble of a World Cup is hard to explain; everything is heightened, including emotions. Gregory and I have always been extremely close and the thought of him not being there was horrible, but worse than that was knowing the disappointment he would be feeling at having to go home. He ended up watching the semi-final and final on TV at a certain Sophie Hemming's house in Bristol. He had never met her before, but she trained with England team mate Kim Oliver and me in Bath and I really wanted Gregory to watch the game with someone else who was somehow connected and would understand the emotional tie. Sophie missed out on making the cut in 2006 but was integral to our campaign in 2010 and the win in 2014. We became training partners and firm friends, but more than that, Sophie became a huge inspiration to me for reasons that will become clear later in this book.

We faced the home nation Canada in the semi-final; a match where we came just centimetres from missing out on the World Cup final. Kim Shaylor, who played on the wing, saved the day by tackling and dislodging the ball into touch from the clutches of Heather Moyse, Canada's winger, the tournament's top point-scorer and all-round athletic star who also competed successfully at bobsleigh. Moyse was striding away down the wing in front of a stand full of home support and was on for a near-certain try. I was too far away to do anything, and I remember my heart just stopped. It was awful. For a millisecond my world came to a complete standstill with the realisation that with only a 4-point cushion our World Cup dreams were about to come crashing down around us. This was not in the plan. But our super, speedy winger Kim Shaylor came to the rescue and by the skin of our teeth we got into the final, winning 10-6.

We lost by 8 points in the final. New Zealand really demonstrated to us the level we needed to be at to win a World Cup. Even though we lost, our forward pack was, I believe, the best in the world then, and throughout the next few years. We just could not pull it all together as a team as well as we should have done in order to win. Graham Smith did a great job as forwards coach with a very special group of players. I have already mentioned Rob Clayton, other names to note in particular were Georgia Stevens and 'T. J.' Sutton. Both of them were world class, and an honour to play alongside.

Looking back, I did not realise the significance of what I was part of at the time, and what it meant. If I could go back in time I would not change the 2006 result, because if we had gone on to win in 2010 it would have meant so much more. It's like nearly losing the guy you are meant to be with after two dates – when you meet him again two years later you understand the significance, you understand how important and how true that love is – and you will read later that I am writing this from personal experience. Winning is only really winning after a loss. Ronan Keating was right; life really is a roller coaster – you need the troughs to understand quite how high the peaks are. (Don't judge me but I used to be a Boyzone fan; my university housemates were sick of me playing 'When the Going Gets Tough' on repeat on my CD player).

When we came home from Canada and we started to assimilate ourselves back into normal life I had to listen to so many people congratulating me because we had come second in the world. It didn't seem right to me that people were saying well done, impressed at our achievement. We didn't achieve; we lost. So whilst some people are happy at winning silver medals, I was distraught at losing gold; to me, at the time, silver was nothing to be celebrated. But time was a healer, and perhaps more significantly so was the opportunity of 'making good'. My thoughts turned from looking back and losing to looking forward to 2010 and the possibility of winning. We were good in 2006, but not good enough. In 2010 we were going to be good enough, we were going to be more than good enough, and we were going to win.

The next four years for me and the team were fantastic – from the final whistle in Edmonton until the starting whistle in London on 5 September 2010, barring a couple of blips, everything was great, really great. Losing a World Cup final, I can tell you, is the biggest motivator for the next four years. No amount of money or perks can come close to leveraging that kind of motivational power.

Four years on in 2010, in front of a sell-out stadium at the Twickenham Stoop at about seventy-seven minutes into the game, and I was sitting on the bench with my head in my hands. I knew we were going to lose and there was nothing I could do about it. I was helpless, watching my dream slip away. I was substituted at seventy minutes. Rugby is definitely a squad game and I strongly believe in tactically using replacements to make an impact, but when it is you who is taken off it is tough. One of the most commonly used video clips for the 2010 Women's Rugby World Cup montages is of exactly that – me sitting with my head in my hands looking distraught, helpless. I used to hate leaving the pitch, especially as captain (and luckily I did not have to experience this much), but even more so in a World Cup final. There was not a single part of me that wanted to leave that pitch; I had had no idea that I was going to be subbed off, and it meant that I could not give everything to the cause. Publicly, until now, it is a decision I have agreed with, but I can now say here that I did not agree with it, and still don't. I am not sure that I would have made that change when we were still in the game, when we had potential to win, when we were drawing 10-all with the reigning World Champions in the World Cup final. Why would I be taken off the pitch? But I was, it was out of my control and the last ten minutes of that game were absolute agony. At 10 all we had an incredible opportunity, but after a penalty was awarded to New Zealand following an England player infringement, the Black Ferns went ahead 13-10 and there was no fighting back.

After the final whistle went time did not seem real. We were going to win, that was the plan, that was going to happen – but no. We had lost by 3 points. The world was a blur but I had one thing on my mind: I had to gather the players. Most were crying, all were devastated; many did not know what to do. We had to collect medals and then watch the Black Ferns lift the trophy, but it was important to me that all the players held their heads high because that is what you do in rugby. You win graciously but you also lose graciously. What followed was probably the toughest couple of hours I have ever had to endure. Very soon after the game and the final whistle I had to leave my team mates to do a live television interview with Sky Sports. I had to walk behind the screen before we went live to wipe my tears away. I didn't want to cry on live television, but it was a real struggle not to. I was the captain and at that moment I had to be as strong as possible for my heartbroken team mates. I just had to keep going.

The route to the final in 2010 had been smooth running for us. With Ireland, Kazakhstan and the USA in our group we knew it would be physical, but I was certain that we would cruise through – though obviously, being the well media-trained captain that I was, I did not say this at the time. Our first pool game was against the Irish, a team who seemed to always be improving and four years later played a very significant part in England's 2014 victory. They remained a team that I never lost to in an England shirt. We beat them 27-nil to kick-start our campaign. Kazakhstan came next and I was rested along with three other players, including Rochelle 'Rocky' Clark. We both hated it but could understand. With only three days between pool games squad rotation was key. I had to watch Sarah Beale, who played 8 in that game, run riot on the pitch and score a try in a game I would have relished playing. Selfishly speaking that was tough, but it was good for the team. We had our shared goal of winning the World Cup so it didn't matter who was playing. The team was bigger than its individuals.

The last pool game against the USA was physically tougher but our class shone out and we won 37-10. Our semi-final was against Australia; we played really well in that game, our selection was good and we got through what could have been a potentially dangerous fixture. Alice Richardson played extremely well at 12, allowing Katy Mclean at 10 just that extra bit of support to play her own game well. I scored the first try at six minutes with Danielle 'Nolli' Waterman scoring our second at twenty-two minutes. Alice Richardson added to the scoring tally in the second half with a penalty and that was job done: 15-nil. We did have a couple of casualties from the game unfortunately; Fi Pocock got smashed into touch in what has become one of the most viewed rugby tackles on YouTube. Fi was now out injured, having damaged pretty much everything she possibly could in her knee. Fi was one of the best players I had the pleasure of taking to the pitch with in an England shirt; she was strong, whilst light of foot and skilful and never, ever made a mistake. One of my highlights was beating her in a one-on-one battle in a training session whilst out at a Nations Cup in Canada in 2009. How did I beat her? Not with strength or size, as might be expected, but with my footwork – not something I was known for, but it was true! Fi has never really managed to make a successful return to international rugby after that tackle. A huge loss of what might have been. We also lost another player – back-row player Heather Fisher, who broke her thumb, but such was the quality of our back row that we still put out a world-class unit even with a player of Heather's calibre out.

My twin brother used to make notes when he was watching me play for England. He got so emotionally involved in the build-up to games and throughout the eighty minutes because his twin sister was out there, that this was the easiest way for him to channel his emotions. He then would write up his thoughts after the game and quite often send them to me. This book includes excerpts of Gregory's notes and write-ups. I have not changed any words; they are all Gregory's, copied from his original notebooks or handwritten bits of paper or typed articles that he sent through to me after games. (Gregory, I will buy you a pint to say thank you!) The first one that I will share describes the 2010 final. I know how hard Gregory would have found it to write this, know how much he would have been wishing that the words could have been different and that this particular story had led to a different conclusion:

*

England lose but win the hearts of a nation.

Oh the agony of sport. The differences between these two sides were small but the result was massively different for both. The New Zealand women, jubilant at the final whistle, will care not for the score or how they did it. They have a gold medal around their necks. For their opposing team, the England women, they were left with a silver medal around their necks, their heavy hearts covered in a cloud of what-ifs. But there is some silver-lining to that cloud. This battle, their courage, their blood, their tears, it will not just be left on the Twickenham Stoop pitch. No, what this wonderful collection of women have done goes beyond the surrounds of this stadium in south-west London. True, they lost, but they have won over a nation with their sheer magnificence, their humility, their modesty. . . there just aren't enough superlatives for this team.

In a pulsating game that had the record-sized crowd gripped from the haka to the final whistle there was little to separate the sides. New Zealand had the more precise kicking game which allowed them to pin England back into their own half and on the day were able to control their own possession a little better. England will rue the errors that they allowed into their game and which continually allowed New Zealand to apply pressure. From the kick-off England knocked on, and from this England barely saw the ball again for the first quarter of the game. But England weathered storm after storm. Surely you felt England's line would break, but time and again they would get a crucial turnover. Unfortunately for England though, they could not create their own pressure and New Zealand's defence was only rarely tested. When England did this the NZ defence infringed. Credit to New Zealand: their ruthlessness never let up and they continually strove to go forward. The pressure eventually told in the 35th minute when Carla Hohepa, Player of the Tournament, got her feet going and skipped over for a try. On the stroke of half-time England had a good drive down field and, with their defence being tested, New Zealand invariably infringed. The penalty came agonisingly close and deflected off the upright. In a sense these inches summed up the game for England. So, so close.

But England came out at half-time and after a succession of pick and drives New Zealand infringe again. This time Mclean made no mistake and brought the score to 7-3. And then came what could have been a seminal moment in the game. Carla Hohepa, who had been scoring tries for fun in this tournament, found herself clear and striding to the try line. But then Jo McGilchrist, her determination an embodiment of this England team, somehow catches and brings Hohepa down on what must be a tackle of a lifetime. Do not forget McGilchrist is a second row. Phenomenal. As ever though, New Zealand continued to pour towards the try line and more vital tackles from Spencer and then a crucial turnover from Maggie Alphonsi somehow kept New Zealand from crossing the whitewash. It was inspirational to watch but heart-breaking to think about with the hindsight of the result. On a different day this defence would have won the game.

Not long later England found themselves under pressure again and this time they were caught infringing. Kelly Brazier stroked the ball over to give the Black Ferns a 10-3 lead. Refusing to let go of the trophy, England came back and put pressure on New Zealand. Once again New Zealand were penalised and Captain Catherine Spencer opted for a scrum five metres from the line. Again, New Zealand infringed and again England went for the scrum. The front row can take credit for the resulting try but Spencer sucked in three defenders before giving the ball to Amy Turner who showed great hands to Charlotte Barras who sliced over to score. Utter jubilation in the crowd, which magnified when Mclean slotted the conversion. 10 all and twenty minutes to go. From the kick-off England give away a penalty and once again put themselves under pressure. With this continual pressure it was inevitable that New Zealand were awarded another penalty and Kelly Brazier once again put this over to give themselves a crucial 3-point lead going into the last fifteen minutes. England needed to get out of their half but too often the kicks went down the throats of the New Zealand back three who always ran back with venom deeply into England's half. And so the time ticked down all too quickly and with Alice Richardson being stretchered off England were left with fourteen players and ultimately ran out of time when the Kiwi scrum-half booted the ball out.

The England team gave everything in this performance. Catherine Spencer, a fine leader of this team, led by example time and again. Rachael Burford did not stop tackling in midfield and Jo McGilchrist put herself everywhere on this pitch. Maggie Alphonsi, who should have received the Player of the Tournament, once again put her body on the line for the entire eighty minutes. I feel for this team, the players, the coaches. The wounds of defeat will heal but scars will always be there. They deserved better than this.

But that is sport. There is always a winner and a loser and unfortunately England found themselves on the wrong side of the scoreboard. But these women are not losers. They are incredible with their dedication, hard work, commitment. They have changed the way the sport is viewed. They have inspired a generation. They are true role models. To anyone who has shared a part of their World Cup journey they will always be champions to us.

We collected our silver medals in front of the crowd, most of whom had stayed to support us and share our sadness. I didn't want my medal. I still don't want it. I know it is in my house in a bag, in a box, hidden away, and it only comes out when I pretend to enjoy showing it to a school assembly or something similar. I don't look at it. But worse than collecting that medal was standing to the side, to make way for the Black Ferns and watch them bouncing up onto the podium, collecting their winner's medals, raising the trophy aloft with cheers and incredibly emotional celebrations. That is the toughest spectacle I have witnessed in my life. I felt numb – but still I could not rest, I could not think.

Streety (Gary Street – head coach) and I then had to go and face the press conference. A room packed full of journalists, cameras, microphones – more media than I had ever faced. I had to talk to them about what happened, about how we lost. I wanted to be anywhere but there, I didn't feel like I could be brave enough, but I was captain, I had to stay strong for my team mates who had no idea what I was currently going through. My team mates who were already with family or close friends. I had to somehow get something positive across; I knew that we only had a small window of media to use to promote our sport.

Women's sport and women's rugby at the time got so little media exposure I was fully aware that we still had to present positive messages. We were always ambassadors for our sport; that never switched off. We were so conscious of it and never more so than prior to, during and following a home World Cup. There really was a feeling that the nation had got behind us during those three short weeks in 2010; it felt like members of the public supported us because we were just normal women. We were daughters, sisters, wives, girlfriends, teachers, students, office workers, vets, policewomen and so on. As my dad always used to say, we were ordinary people doing extraordinary things. And yes, we did achieve something – we ensured that England's rugby team were in another World Cup final, and we did nearly win in a game that was heralded at the time as the greatest match in women's rugby to date. That is not bad, I guess, but it was not good enough.

In 2007 the England men's team were awarded Team of the Year at the Sports Personality of the Year awards after losing in the World Cup final against South Africa. I remember speaking to their coach Brian Ashton that night; he said that he felt embarrassed that the team were picking up the award. I know what he meant; at that time, the women's team rarely got any national recognition for our successes, although if we had done after the final in 2010 I wouldn't have wanted it. We will always know as players, and I will always know as captain, that we should have won that game. People were congratulating us because we came second in the world, but I was mourning because we lost. Basic errors, missed kicks, not adapting quickly enough on the pitch, some poor decision-making, the wrong tactics, perhaps the wrong selection? Team selection felt right in the semi-final but not quite so right for the final when it was changed in the centres. I would have kept Alice Richardson at 12 to support Katy Mclean at 10. Our kicking game in the semi-final against Australia was spot on because of this, but I don't think it was in the final. I don't exactly know – I have never forced myself to relive the nightmare by watching that game again. But I know without doubt that we could and should have won that game.

I also know, and perhaps this is harder to take, that if the 2010 World Cup had followed the same route and pattern as the 2014 World Cup we would have won. Or that if the same 2010 team had taken to the field in 2014 against the same opposition we would have won. But in rugby we don't think like this, this way of thinking does not adhere to our values, which I wholeheartedly buy into. But I have written these words, no one else. I am finding it very difficult not to think these thoughts and it is tearing me apart.

Before the post-match press conference, I went back to the changing room to get changed. At least, I must have done but I have no recollection of this whatsoever. I don't remember leaving the pitch after the presentation, I don't remember going into the changing room, I don't remember speaking to any of my team mates. I think I was in shock because what was meant to happen during our eighty minutes on the pitch hadn't happened. What we had worked towards, what we had trained for, our goal that we had not swayed from over the last four years, was not met.

After the press conference the next thing I do remember with any clarity is experiencing the strongest urge just to be with my family. They were in the main bar of the Stoop along with several hundred other supporters. It felt like an absolute age to finally get to my family, because supporters, fans and friends wanted to speak to me or hug me or just stare and work out how I was feeling, but when I finally got there I could only cry. I felt so bad for my parents and brothers; I felt so bad for myself. What was I meant to do or think? What were my parents meant to do or think? Out of the corner of my eye I saw a group of the Black Ferns parading the trophy. I felt sick. My family left an hour or so after that, feeling gutted for me, for themselves; I know my twin brother, especially, was feeling a lot of my pain. There was an after-party for all the World Cup squads that night but family were not allowed in. They were the only people I wanted to be with; why on earth would I want to go to a party? But we had no choice, we had to go, so that night we did what all good rugby players do: we got drunk, beer-fuelled laughter disguising our hurt for just a few hours longer.

Very early the next morning Maggie Alphonsi and I had to get up at stupid o'clock to make an appearance on Sky Sports breakfast news. After about two hours' sleep and bribed by the promise of a bacon sarnie and mug of tea, we did a pretty good job, I think. Even in our hungover, depressed, numb, shocked state we were still acutely aware of our jobs as ambassadors. Jobs that Maggie and I have continued to carry out ever since that day and into retirement. The next day I still could not go home – I had to appear in a post-World Cup feature for Sky Sports Rugby. It was filmed at my then-boyfriend's flat in Surrey. Mel Platt, a Sky Sports rugby reporter at the time, came round with the film crew along with a whole bunch of newspapers to trawl through. It was yet another job to get through whilst balancing precariously between showing too much emotion and not enough. I have been attempting to master the art of this ever since, toppling over and mis-balancing on some occasions. One example was when I attended a function at Frome Rugby Club in Somerset where Sarah Hunter ('Sunts') was the speaker. I sat listening to her describe her 2014 World Cup victory with tears rolling down my face – hidden from most people by the darkness of the room but spotted by Sunts – someone I had played alongside in the back row many times, and who wore the 8 shirt that was so special to me in the 2014 final.

After filming finished on the day after the World Cup I finally went home to my own flat. I had not been there for nearly three months and I could not wait to sleep in my big double bed again. It was a place of comfort that I craved so much during this time of such hurt and pain: my bed, my space where I was me; I was not Catherine Spencer – World Cup losing captain – I was just me. I had a bath and got into bed, only to see a couple of yards away on my carpet the biggest spider I had ever seen in England, and it was in my flat in Bristol, in my bedroom, two yards away from my cosy comfort. I may have just played number 8 in the World Cup final, I may have put my body on the line for my team mates, I may have gone to the limit physically and mentally, but there was no way on this earth that I could possibly sleep in the same room as that spider. I tried to telepathically encourage Mr Spider to leave the room from behind the safety of my duvet (it is an absolute fact that duvets protect you from everything), but Mr Spider was not budging.

The desire to sleep in my own bed at this point still far outweighed my fear of Mr Spider, so I reluctantly moved away from the all-protecting duvet and went to fetch my spider removal kit: a pint glass and a piece of card, washing-up gloves and a pair of walking boots. Back into the bedroom I went – now wearing my protective walking boots – to have it out with Mr Spider. I managed to edge closer, mustering all my courage to get within arm's reach. I was a millisecond away from conquering my opposition when he jumped at the last minute and won the battle – he was obviously a Kiwi spider. He darted past me and ran behind the wardrobe out of reach, out of touch. With tears in my eyes at the frustration of the situation, at being forced to surrender to Mr Spider, I withdrew and moved to the spare room. My first night back in my home was not spent in my lovely big double bed but in the little single bed in the spare room. Typical.

For the next few days I did very little. I just tried to get through the days, to get from morning to night. On some days, little tasks such as walking to the local shop to buy milk and bread were a challenge too far. But I had to face reality. Life goes on, and I had a new job to start with the Rugby Football Union for Women (as it was then), working as a women's and girls' development manager in the south-west of England. No escaping from rugby or the women's rugby community. No escape from my heartache. I also had to go back to club training at Bristol. I remember that I started back at the same time as Sophie Hemming. We drove to the club together and sat in the car for a while before getting out and facing our team mates. Neither of us particularly wanted to get out of the safety of the enclosed car. Why? I felt nervous, ashamed and guilty for not winning. I felt like I had let my rugby community down. But out of the car we got, and headed back into the warm, friendly environment of Bristol Ladies rugby. I was not captain there, so I was able to shrink into the background a little. With work I did not have that option.

My role as a women's rugby development manager was to increase participation in the women's and girls' game across Cornwall, Devon, Somerset and Gloucestershire. A tough job made tougher by virtually zero budget and a minuscule percentage of access to the RFU community rugby coach resource, which was scarce enough across the south-west region for RFU staff let alone for women and girls. But actually, the volunteers in the south-west were great. Because they didn't expect much in the way of resources from Twickenham, they just got on with projects themselves. My job was also made harder due to some pretty poor relationship-building prior to my time in post. One of the biggest parts of the job was to get the county officers onside but also to get the RFU staff onside, and I quickly learned how important it was to choose your battles. I had the advantage that I was the England captain, and that title made it easier to go to meetings and start to repair some damaged bridges. In 2010 the coverage of the game had increased so much that the wider rugby community did a strange thing. They started to not just accept women's rugby but to actually at times respect us. But this meant for the few months after not achieving my dream, our dream, I had to relive this every day as I was going out into the community to talk about my experience. How could I heal like this?

I remember going on a school visit – not part of my job description but I've never been good at saying no – where I had to go around to several classes talking about the World Cup. I was asked to take in my medal and show it off. I could hardly bear to touch it at the time, but the kids loved it and were in complete awe. Well, most of them. One boy put his hand up at question time and said, 'That medal is silver – that meant you lost.' I hope to this day that that particular young boy did not see the tears rapidly build up in my eyes. Luckily that was the last question, time was up and I could get out of that room. Horrific. Now I am happy to deliver school assemblies, and I do it a lot. Back then it was just reliving the nightmare, but I put on my brave face and just got on with it – because I was not just Catherine Spencer; I was Catherine Spencer England Rugby Captain. And that is what makes the life of an elite sportsperson tough – it's not the physical strain or pushing your body to the limit, it's not the pressure of everyday life, being organised and managing time, nor the nutrition – it's the fact that you become a product. A product that people expect a part of, a product that people expect to garner the precious time of, a product that anybody and anyone expects to extract emotion from. Worst of all was that I was also treating myself as a product. I was putting pressure on myself to make player appearances for free, to go above and beyond, not just in my RFU role but also in my personal life, because of what I was – when really what

I should have been doing was allowing myself not just the luxury of time but the necessity of time to grieve following the 2010 loss.

Why does it matter so much? Why was I experiencing so much hurt when all I had actually done was run around a grass pitch for eighty minutes and not get as many points on the board as the opposition? Why, so many years later, does this still plague me? What was I trying to prove? Who was I doing all this for?

I led a selfish life in my quest to win a World Cup, and when we didn't win in 2010 it magnified and exemplified this selfishness, a personality trait that I hate. I was feeling guilty that I had devoted all of this time, emotion and hard work to a dream that never became a reality. I sacrificed an altogether different, perhaps more successful, life that did not involve rugby but instead had the possibility of a good career and financial security. Above all I was following this damn tough path to achieve something and in my own eyes I had failed. I won six Six Nations tournaments, I played in two World Cup finals, I won England Player of the Year, I was recognised by the Rugby Union Writers' Association with an award, I won European tournaments and Nations Cups – but to me I have failed. I earned sixty-three caps for England and lost just eight games, two of which were World Cup finals: a win percentage of 87 per cent; a win percentage of 90 per cent if you remove the World Cup finals from the equation; and a win percentage of 93 per cent as captain. A pretty good return in anyone's book – but not mine. Because we did not win the World Cup when we really should have done. I failed myself and I failed my family, and because of that it was difficult to regain the purpose in my life. How would I find it again, where would I find it, could I find it on my own or did I need help? And why could I not just be normal? Why did I have to go and become England captain? If I could go back in time and start over again, would I make the same life decisions? I don't know. I really don't know.

Chapter Two

The Early Years

On 5 March 2004 at approximately 2:20 p.m. I was stood at the side of the pitch at the Twickenham Stoop, wearing the white shorts and shirt of the England rugby team, with the red rose (well, kind of a rose – more of a tulip for us girls back then, but more of that later) on my chest. My name had been called out and I was about to take to the pitch. This was my moment. This was my reason for being.

I started playing a version of rugby at about the age of five; the game involved high levels of contact, aggression and leg drive. The pitch was the landing at home, my team mate and opposition my two brothers, and the ball a pair of my dad's rolled up chunky socks hand-knitted by his mum, Granny Spencer. Normally Gregory and I were on one team while our older brother, Martin, made up the opposition. Martin was much bigger than us at the time so this was entirely fair. The sport of 'Landing Rugby' was formed and my pick-and-go training commenced. We were not big on developing laws and meddling with the game too much (Landing Rugby is not governed by World Rugby) so we had two laws and two laws only: get the socks to the other end of the landing by any means possible, and stop your opposition by any means possible. I have, ever since, always loved the art of close-quarter rugby. The pick and go, body management in contact, the bear-hug tackle are all favourites of mine, and although so many people talk of free-flowing rugby and the need for more tries, for me there is nothing more beautiful on a rugby pitch than a well-formed driving maul. Anyone who has ever heard me commentate will know this and the title of this book is continued testament to my appreciation and devotion to the maul!

Whilst my brothers graduated from Landing Rugby and went off to mini rugby on a Sunday morning at our local club, Folkestone, which my Dad also played for, I flitted for a while between Sunday School and ballet. I persevered with ballet for a term or so, but it was clear that at age seven I already had the flexibility of an old-school number 8 forward, so it really was not the sport for me. For those of you who are not entirely aware of what the flexibility of a number 8 forward is, let us just say that touching my knees with my hands was a challenge – let alone my toes! I still clearly remember walking along the canal bank with my mum in Hythe, our home town, telling her that I didn't want to carry on with ballet. The look of relief on her face was evident and clear to me even at that young age. Our first performance was coming up and the very precise list specifying the exact types of tutu, hairbands, ballet pumps and so on was rather long and no doubt expensive too. I hung my ballet pumps up and never looked at them again.

A couple of years later I was hankering after something to do, so the almost unheard-of decision was made that I,

Catherine Mary Spencer, a nine-year-old girl, would play rugby. I had a bit of a head start from my Landing Rugby experience; I had also watched my brothers a little bit and, although I struggle to remember now, during the first few years of my life I was on the side of the pitch many times while my dad played. My mum would have been on a neighbouring pitch playing hockey and my brother and I were planted in the middle in our pushchair. Some sporting knowledge must have seeped in. Even so, I was pretty nervous heading up to the club to start training, but my brother was by my side, which made things a whole lot easier, and even though I was a girl I felt like a full part of the team soon enough. It did take a while for me to find my rugby-playing boots though; I remember delivering a forward pass in one of my first training sessions. What was I thinking?

The first time that I remember accepting that I could actually play occurred whilst I was representing the team at a minis' festival. My dad and my older brother were there watching; Gregory and I were on the pitch. I was playing on the wing and suddenly I was thrust into the action. The opposition kicked what at the time felt like a huge 'up and under'. Time stood still as I saw this ball travelling towards my side of the pitch. It was becoming more and more apparent that I was going to have to do something. I would have to catch the ball. I remember getting my arms into position to ensure that I could securely and safely receive the ball into the breadbasket area, as one of our rugby coaches, John McPartlin, used to describe it. Not snatching at the ball with just our hands but getting our whole body behind the ball. I was ready and the ball dropped neatly in to my arms. What to do next? I looked up and I just ran. I ran for most of the length of the pitch (albeit a mini-rugby pitch) before passing to one of my team mates, Adam Tarr, who crossed the line for a try. That was the day that I realised I could play rugby. I was starting to gain confidence through experience. That was the day that my dad also realised that his baby girl could play rugby.

At my club, Folkestone, awards were dished out at the end of each season for the minis section. Gregory had amassed a bit of a collection, but one year it was my turn too. In 1991, in my last season for Folkestone Minis, I was awarded the under-twelves' 'most improved player'. This was no real surprise in some ways, as I had been particularly rubbish when I first started, but the fact that the award was given to a girl was pretty big news. My coaches at the time were brilliant and pretty influential, particularly Mike O'Sullivan, who perhaps had more of an impact on my career than he may have thought. Mike really fought my corner; I was the member of his squad who he felt should win the award and so he was nominating me – no issue. Or was there? Several members of the club were a little surprised at the nomination and wondered what on earth was the point of presenting an award to a girl. What would that achieve? Mike pushed and pushed and I was awarded the trophy. A trophy that I am very proud of and still have nearly thirty years later, albeit stuck together with Sellotape. Here are Mike's own words, when writing for the club newsletter a few years later in 2008:

I coached Catherine for her last two seasons in the juniors. She blossomed into a really talented player and became a valued, popular, respected and fully integrated member of the team. At the end of the season I decided that she merited the 'most improved player' award, supported by the joint coach Mike Linden. A father of a team member commented that this was just tokenism which resulted in my having an unsatisfactory conversation with him (he has been eating a lot of humble pie recently). Catherine received this award purely on merit; indeed she was in close contention for 'best player'. I feel quite proud to have had an input in her success, as must the other coaches.

I think it is important to clarify here that Folkestone became one of the most supportive clubs of women's rugby, are one of the friendliest, most welcoming clubs I have ever experienced (and I have been to a few) and will always have a special place in my heart. It really was worth giving that award to a girl; that little bit of confidence kept me going until I was able to don my boots once more a few years later when Folkestone started a ladies' team. And my first England shirt is hanging on the wall of Folkestone Rugby Club along with a small photo in the bottom left-hand corner of the frame showing me playing rugby aged ten! In 2008 I was awarded the club's very first honorary life Vice Presidency and I love this! I still regularly go up to the club; one of the most heart-warming things about rugby is the understanding and attachment that elite players have for 'grassroots' clubs. I fear that with the emergence of academies in the professional game this humility and understanding will start to wane. I really hope not.

*

At the age of eleven I had to stop playing rugby. Regulations of the game, that I wholeheartedly agree with, prevented me from continuing to play in the boys' team. I was fed up that I would not be able to play for a while but I had played enough to be hooked. I was 100 per cent certain that I would put on my rugby boots again at some point in the future, but I understood that I would have to satisfy my sporting needs in other ways until such time that I was able to play my beloved sport again. I did enjoy playing other sports, but as in rugby there were also barriers in place sometimes. At junior school, I fought my corner to attend cricket practice; until this point girls were not allowed and my request to join in was initially refused, but I kept on at the headmaster who ran the cricket club. I went and asked him week after week until he finally succumbed. So off I went to one practice session and I ran someone out when I hit the stumps whilst fielding in spectacular fashion (underarm of course – I was a girl). I revelled in my own glory for a short while but then decided that I didn't particularly like cricket practice – I had proved my point and didn't need to go again. I do now, however, enjoy watching cricket and *Test Match Special* is one of the best things on the radio. Long may it continue!

At secondary school, at one time or another, I represented my school team at athletics (discus), cross-country (horrific), basketball (in which I also earned a coaching award), rounders, netball, hockey and tennis. Away from school I learned to sail, I did my Duke of Edinburgh Award, I went to Brownies then graduated to Guides and I also spent a fair bit of time in the music department. I achieved my grade eight French horn and played in various orchestras and bands and, unbelievably if you could hear me now, sang in several school choirs including the chamber choir, which involved an actual audition. My life was pretty full but, importantly, it was enjoyable. My parents were great, we were encouraged to take part in different activities, but we were never pushed – the perfect balance – and for this I, and my brothers, have a huge amount to thank our parents for. Then rugby came back into my life, a little earlier than I was expecting, and although I had been prepared to wait until I was older to play again, luckily I didn't have to.

Chapter Three

The Mountain Ascent

It was 1993 and I was at home one evening when my dad came and showed me the local paper. He was pointing at a small article that immediately made me smile. I remember looking up at him with a massive grin on my face. Folkestone Rugby Club were starting a ladies' team and new players were welcome. Off I went to the club the following week and there I remained for several years. Prior to starting at Folkestone, I had gone along to Canterbury Rugby Club for a training session with their ladies' team. I remember that I wore my dad's old university rugby shirt, with the number 8 peeling off the back. I am sure I would have played for them if the opportunity at my local club had not arisen. Canterbury was thirty minutes up the road, pretty close in women's rugby terms, but playing for Folkestone meant so much more.

Although my dad was a member of the club, it took seeing the news in the local paper for me to become aware of the opportunity to play there again, a paper that continued to support our team, and me personally, through various articles over the years. I was fourteen but this time the lack of regulations in women's rugby favoured my age. I did not have to be eighteen to play, so I played senior rugby straight away and continued to play competitive rugby for the next twenty-four years – so all in all a rugby 'career' of over twenty-five years including my mini-rugby years. My first senior game was with my local club, my last ever game of rugby was playing for England Legends against Ireland Legends during the 2017 World Cup. There were, however, several steps in between.

We had been training for a few weeks with various members of the club stepping in to help coach before we got a proper dedicated coach. It was getting towards the end of the season and we were due to play our first fixture. I remember now that the night before felt like Christmas Eve; I was so incredibly excited I could hardly sleep. I woke up in the morning raring to go – unusual for me – only to find out that the opposition had cancelled. I was devastated and had to wait several months before we finally played our first fixture, against another Kent team, Thanet, on a cold, wet, muddy Sunday at Folkestone. We had what felt like a huge crowd coming to cheer us on. Most of the spectators were initially there out of curiosity and probably just to watch thirty women run around in shorts in the mud! But soon enough they realised that we could actually play a little bit and that we kind of knew what we were doing. We won that game 8-5. On the Thursday I excitedly walked to the corner shop and picked up the local weekly paper to read the match report. This became a very familiar Sunday to Thursday routine that continued for several years. Playing the game on the weekend and waiting four days to read the write-up. The headline for our first report in the local paper was A NEW MEANING TO THE MUD PACK and the photo caption started 'At least they had a man in charge . . .' referring to the referee. I am not sure what I feel about those headlines now, but what I can say is that the local papers, whether the *Kent Messenger* or the *Folkestone Herald*, were brilliant supporters of Folkestone Ladies and of me personally. It was something that, looking back, I took for granted at the time; I didn't fully understand that this amount of press, even at a local level, was not normal. The report went on to say:

> Many weeks of hard training paid off with a narrow but deserved win for Folkestone Ladies in their first ever match. A big crowd turned up, the rain was there – all that was missing was a full Thanet side – but the hosts let three players out on loan and a twelve-a-side game was completed. Folkestone dominated the opening half, all of which was played in opposition territory, and excellent work by Catherine Spencer, Amanda Eede, Lucy Baldwin and Amanda Howland kept up the relentless pressure.

My first mention in print! I still remember being really excited by this and I couldn't wait to read the next match report. The amazing reports did continue but so too did the innuendos; in a report about a local derby game the first line read 'Will Carling and Jeremy Guscott had better watch out – because the girls are here and ready to grab some balls!' Classic local-media journalism, but this at least was accompanied by a good photo and nearly half-page feature on the back cover of the sport section – prime spot.

This local coverage really helped the development of our club and to build awareness that women did play rugby.

At that first fixture on that cold, wet Sunday one spectator and member of the club apparently told my Dad that he thought that one day I would play for England – what a thought.

I absolutely loved my time playing for Folkestone. I owe so much to the club who set me on my way. Without them I would still have played, no doubt at Canterbury, where I may have made other friends, but I was so motivated to play for England whilst representing my local club that once the opportunity was there I was not going to go anywhere else. There was a brief half-season when I succumbed to pressure to play for a premiership club and travelled to Richmond, but I was not yet ready or confident enough for this move, so I headed back to Folkestone; Folkestone was my club through and through. My Richmond experiment knocked my confidence hugely at the time and was not a nice experience. I strongly believe that every player should be taken in context; a blanket rule that subsequently came into force that everyone should play premiership rugby if they want to play for England is, in principle, good, but the odd gem might be missed.

Seeing Folkestone RFC listed as my club on the England programmes was awesome, and it was the prospect of this tiny little thing that drove me on. Folkestone, apart from being my first club, was the club where my dad played and the club where my two brothers played and the club where some of my best mates played and the club that we used to head up to every year a few days before Christmas when we were little to get presents from 'Father Christmas'; it was the club where we used to go every November to watch the firework display, the club where, aged thirteen, I enjoyed my first 'slow dance', with a boy at a club French exchange trip party; it was the club I went on to enjoy many tours with when I was a little older (what happens on tour stays on tour). It represented so much, and I loved playing for England while playing for Folkestone. I became the player and leader that I did because of this, but it did mean that I had to fight a little harder, emotionally, in order to get there. I went from being big fish in a little pond to relatively small fish in a massive ocean, an ocean that was scary but full of possibilities.

It was in my second season of my senior rugby career that I made the first real step up my rugby mountain. I always describe my rugby career as a series of false summits, and really that was exactly what it was. When I first started playing rugby I didn't know much at all about England women's rugby and, to be honest, when I won that mini's 'most improved' award in 1989, England's women's team barely existed. A Great Britain team played a test against France in 1986 and England played their first test, I believe, in 1987 against Wales, but I had no knowledge of this at the time. My dream at that point was not to play rugby for England; it was simply to play. At first I didn't know that anything existed above club rugby, but as time passed I began to see something above me. I thought I was at the top of my mountain, only to see when I got there that there was still something higher. This happened at every level until I eventually made it to national level. But even then, this process did not stop. I was always looking up, and I always wanted to go higher, but I was far from certain that I should be there or deserved to be there. I was just a girl from Folkestone playing for her local club. I was trekking far from my roots and I was not sure if I was allowed on that path with the other people who were there. I felt that if I looked up I would see a big arrow pointing at me with the word 'Imposter'. Imposter syndrome is something that I talk about now when delivering speeches to businesses. It is a phrase bandied about a lot in the corporate world but it is not just business speak. It is real and exists and I have lived with it for a very long time. I still feel it now. What am I, still just that girl from Folkestone, even doing writing this book? Imposter, fraud, someone will find me out.

In that second full season, I remember sitting at home one evening in the front room with my parents and my brothers, not knowing that I was about to face my first big summit. The phone rang and it was for me; it was my rugby coach Jon Turbutt. Jon was our first long-term coach at Folkestone and he was brilliant. He pushed us when needed, congratulated us when deserved and always came up with fun, interesting training sessions. I loved every minute of training. The reason Jon was phoning me was to ask me to attend trials for the Kent county squad. Wow. I was excited, nervous, proud – I went along to the trials and got into the squad. It felt so great to represent my county. Remember, at that stage I still didn't have any idea that an England women's team existed. I loved rugby, watched England men on TV and by family association was an avid Bath supporter, due to the fact that I had a West Country father hailing from Trowbridge. But women's rugby was not on TV or in the news at all. I didn't know about any elite level rugby for women. I had no clue, but what I did know was that I was going to represent my county. I thought I had made it! So, in the 1996–97 season, at the age of seventeen I was selected to play for the senior Kent ladies' team along with two other players from Folkestone. Unfortunately, one of my two team mates was unable to play, so Amanda Eede and I represented Folkestone for the first time in the women's county set-up. I felt really proud that I was representing my club at a higher level alongside players from other clubs across the county.

My first Kent game was played at Teddington in Surrey. I was incredibly nervous. I didn't know anyone in the squad apart from Amanda, and they certainly did not know me. Before we played, we had to remove the deer from the pitch, probably a nice distraction in the build-up to the game. I played second row, and was excited to be donning the navy-blue Kent shirt. Years later I was the first female to be recognised with a Kent Rugby service to rugby award. I was presented with a silk scarf at a Vice President's lunch at Folkestone. Apparently, it took a whole Kent committee meeting to decide what I should be presented with. Ties were the standard award, so the committee had to put their thinking caps on! I still have the scarf, along with my other rugby memorabilia: I'm proud of my Kent roots. To be honest I don't remember much about that first game but I went on to play several games for Kent at different stages in my career and loved it.

One of my favourite games for Folkestone, and the moment when I really knew that I loved the game, was when we played against Canterbury, the team that I could have ended up playing for. Folkestone Ladies had been going for just a couple of seasons, and Canterbury were at the time one of the strongest set-ups in the country. The referee blew for time early, just before Canterbury scored 100 unanswered points against us, but despite this I came off the pitch buzzing; I remember dancing around the changing room after the game, telling my team mates that I just wanted to go straight back out there. I am not sure that they shared my enthusiasm at that particular point! After the famous Canterbury loss we kept working hard, at times with summer training numbers dropping as low as four or five players, but we kept going and became one of the most successful teams in the south-east, overtaking Canterbury who were dropping, rising up through the ranks, gaining promotion several years running and making it to Division One – just below the national championship.

One of our close Cup games saw us play against the Trojans, a team that are still going strong. When we played them the light (or lack of it) was in our favour. We were drawn at full-time but as there were no floodlights available we could not play extra time, so as the away team we were awarded the win. I still remember the game now and the desire to win outright was huge. We came back from behind and scored in the last play, which saw us progress in the Cup. And I loved the write-up that came out a few days later. I can still picture my dad reading it and grinning massively!

. . . Folkestone started well and Bec Hawley's huge kick took them close to the home line from where they drove through for Mags MacArthur to open the scoring. But Trojans dominated the scrums and released their powerful backs to lead by 12-5 by half-time. Folkestone battled hard, but just when they seemed to be gaining the initiative, the home side broke away to increase their lead by a further 5 points. Feeling on the touchline was that this was Trojans' day, but Folkestone soon set out to prove them wrong. They had fire and determination. And they had the truly formidable Catherine Spencer. Constant breaks off the scrums and mauls by the number 8 forward, with support from all the forwards, saw Folkestone gaining enormous ground. . .

I loved that game. Individually I played well, and of course I was pleased about that and was gaining confidence, but mainly I enjoyed winning with Folkestone and the rest of the team. Another match report, following another victory for Folkestone, read: 'Catherine Spencer had yet another fine game spending much of the afternoon shrugging off challenges, tackling and collecting the ball well, running through the middle of the opposition or chasing up the wing to score a total of six tries.' I was starting to find that I was enjoying the limelight, and with that, most importantly, came increasing confidence. I was starting to believe. In what I thought was going to be my last game for Folkestone, before my abortive stint at Richmond, the last few sentences of the match report read:

The game really belonged to Catherine Spencer playing in her last game for Folkestone before moving on to play at a higher level with Richmond. She scored four tries in this game and dominated play throughout the game. The forwards and the rest of the team responded well to her surging runs. Catherine will be missed but we all look forward to one day perhaps watching her play in an England shirt.

Expectation was building!

Chapter Four
The Interloper

The next key phase of my rugby development was at university. There were not many universities that offered the course I wanted to study, Philosophy and Sociology, but Cardiff was one of them. I had never been to the city, so in 1997 I went along with my dad for a weekend to see what it was like. The course would be fine, but I wanted to see what it would feel like to live there. Of course, we tied in an opportunity to watch some rugby, so on the Saturday afternoon we travelled farther west to Stradey Park, Llanelli, where the England women's team were taking on Wales in what was then the Home Nations, a precursor to the Five Nations that later became the Six Nations.

It was the first women's international fixture that I had watched, and it felt good to be in the stand despite being in a very stark minority of English fans in the very Welsh stadium. This was the first time I saw Gill Burns in action. She was captain and number 8 and directed the game so well. England camped on the line for the last period of the game, with Burnsie controlling things at the back of the scrum. England won, and in fact won every fixture against Wales until 2009, at a match when yours truly was in the thick of it. Not a good day at the office that day. Back in 1997, though, England were victorious, and just after the final whistle had been blown I found myself in the middle of the pitch – very grudgingly. The players were still on the pitch, so my dad seized his opportunity to see if I was big enough to one day play international rugby. I was so embarrassed. He made me go down and stand on the pitch near the players so that he could size us up. I was trying to be subtle but he kept making me step closer so that I was practically rubbing shoulders with the players. He didn't need to worry – I was always one of the bigger players.

When I packed my bags and headed to Cardiff later that year, little did I know that they had one of the best university rugby teams in the country. I still remember nervously going up to the women's rugby table at the freshers' fair. They asked me to fill out a form and I saw their eyes light up when I noted down that I had already played county rugby. In the late 1990s it was much more common for women to first pick up a ball at university than to turn up already a seasoned player.

I played second row in my first season of university rugby and moved to the back row in my second year. In my first and second year our captain was a player called Kesner Ridge and she was awesome. She was then and still is now the best captain I have ever played under. Her presence and aura both on and off the pitch were spot on. She was one of those captains who you just wanted to play well for. Your own ambition disappeared – it was all about playing well for Kes. She used to deliver these incredible team talks that made everyone in the room feel ten feet taller, ten seconds faster. Everyone in the room had a purpose and was vital for the success of the team. Her captaincy inspired me and a bit of Kes was always with me before club games or university games or even England games and whenever I was captain. I lost contact with her after I left university, so I really hope that she is reading this now and understands the impact that she had on me as both a player and future captain.

The first time I played at Twickenham was when I was representing Cardiff University. We won the regional Welsh university competition stage very easily to qualify for the final national knockout tournament. We glided through the pool stages with relative ease, beating Leeds University along the way. We then played Edinburgh in the final on the oh-so-hallowed turf. My dad and my uncle came to watch, along with a group of my old school friends, which was great. This was, however, when I commenced my training for losing in finals, as we missed out on the title by 2 points. We were gutted but we made it back to Cardiff that evening to celebrate our Twickenham experience in the student union nonetheless. Kesner Ridge won Player of the Match, extremely impressive for a player from the losing team.

We got our revenge against Edinburgh the following year, though, in the quarter-final of the 1998–99 BUSA championship, beating them 19-14 on their home ground. It was a really long day, and the uncomfortable journey home for me made it feel even longer. In this match (this was before the days of law changes around the ruck area)

I was on the receiving end of the most ferocious rucking I have ever experienced. After making a tackle and generally making a nuisance of myself in the ruck I found myself on the wrong side. I wanted to move (I really did) but I saw three pairs of large Scottish boots come towards me at pace and I was actually scared – the only time I was ever scared on a rugby pitch. I remember just curling up in a ball, covering my head and trying not to cry. I couldn't do anything other than hope that the referee would blow his whistle and come to my rescue. He did finally whistle to award a penalty against me. This was exactly the right decision; I had been on the wrong side and this was the best lesson for me.

When I got back to Cardiff after sitting sideways on a ropy old bus for about seven hours and after a few beers (obviously!) I showed my housemates my battle scars. Their immediate reaction was to tell me to go to A&E to get stitches. I didn't because I had other things to do and I was a rugby player and we didn't tend to do that kind of thing unless our leg was actually hanging off. I was proud of my war wounds – wounds I'd got through a pair of thick old school rugby shorts and thick cycling shorts under that. Both shorts were ripped to shreds, as were the backs of my legs.

In the semi-final we were drawn against Loughborough University and we played the match at Banbury Rugby Club. My dad and my older brother Martin came to watch the game. We lost narrowly, which meant we just missed out on progressing to Twickenham that year. I will never forget watching a distraught Kes walk away from the pitch arm in arm with her father at the end of the game. I felt that we had let her down. I wanted to win for myself but more than that I wanted us to win for Kes and for the team. I was not important. In my third year I captained the side, doing my best to fill the massive shoes of Kes.

This was the year I was also asked to captain the Welsh Universities team. This was an invitational side made up of the best players selected from all of the university teams in Wales. At the time I was surprised to be asked but I was also truly honoured. While I loved playing for Welsh Universities, it did feel a bit tough when we played against England Students (a team I had trialled for but didn't get into), and I had to remember to refer to my team as Wales rather than my home country. As Welsh Universities we again made a long trip to Edinburgh, to play Scottish Students. We won what was an incredibly close game and I still remember looking over to see our coaches jumping up and down with excitement. I will never forget it. I guess it was a glimpse of what it was like to play for the Lions: players who are normally in strict opposition to each other coming together and growing a bond that is so tight and close. I loved it. Our post-match drinking was probably also similar to the proper Lions teams of old too. After our awesome victory the beers flowed well, and after several hours in various pubs and bars one of my team mates and I decided that it would be a really good idea if we got a train to Inverness. We left the bar without telling anyone (because that would be funnier when they couldn't find us) and somehow found our way to the station. I am thankful that our far-from-efficient stumbling meant that we had just missed the last train. We went back to the bar, rejoined the team and they were none the wiser.

During my time at university I also stepped up to regional rugby level and represented South-East England. It was then that I really started to feel like I was getting closer to something amazing. At this time there was still something called divisional rugby as the next step above regional rugby. One of my first appearances for South-East England, if not the first, was on 28 November 1999 as part of a Regional and Divisional Championships day. Two regional matches took place followed by the divisional match. I was on the bench for the South-East Region. My dad had come to watch and after my game we walked over to watch the Midlands v South divisional match. There were some impressive names on both team sheets and some that I came to know much better and even played alongside. For the South Maxine Edwards, T. J. Sutton, Georgia Stevens and Susie Appleby were just a few key names and for the Midlands Jo Yapp and Karen Andrew running the show at 9 and 10. Watching these players on that day inspired me; I wanted to be like them and a small part of me felt that I was good enough. I was gaining confidence through the experience of others: to be able to see others playing, to be able to see what you want to aim for, is invaluable and is one of the reasons why it is so important to have more women's rugby shown on TV.

After university I went away travelling with my twin brother for a year. By this time I was aware that an England women's rugby team existed but it didn't feel important enough to miss out on a year travelling with Gregory. I felt that I could come back to rugby on my return. I knew I was going to play club rugby again, but it took the year away for me to really decide that I wanted to go higher up the rugby mountain. That spark of inspiration watching the Divisional players remained with me through my year away and kept the fire burning until I came home. If I could turn back the clock now I would have still done exactly the same thing. I experienced one of the best years of my life with my twin brother.

Very soon after I returned home in 2002 my Folkestone coach, Woody, told me about some regional summer academy trials that were taking place. I was not at my fittest but went along and did enough to get into the summer training programme – the next step up my mountain, heading towards the next summit. Driving to my first session I was incredibly nervous; then as I got closer I could see the pitch and my heart sank. It was evident that a female coach was leading the session. It is hard to describe my feeling and I am sure it will be questioned by many who read this, but I did then what others do now: I thought because she was female she would not be good enough. That coach was Giselle Mather, one of the best coaches in the country and a former England international. She was incredible and certainly snapped my irrational feelings back into correct shape. The way she engaged players, pushed at times, nurtured and supported at others, was the perfect balance. She was innovative, always thinking in detail about what she was delivering rather than issuing drills just because they had been used by coaches before her.

Giselle went on to be part of the coaching team for the 2006 World Cup; she then left women's rugby and worked for London Irish as part of their academy. I spoke to male players who had been coached by her there and they could not speak highly enough of her. Giselle is now back coaching in the women's game at Wasps – this is great for the game but masks a frustrating end to her time at London Irish; I have no doubt that a 'glass ceiling' of sorts exists for female coaches in the men's game. Giselle is by far one of the best coaches in the country and if she was a man I am sure she would have got to a higher coaching level than she did during her time at Sunbury.

That year I spent most of the summer feeling terrified and incredibly nervous leading up to training days. I didn't really feel confident that I was good enough to be there, but something drove me on. I had a quiet determination that did not completely disappear, although it was nearly beaten down by my lack of self-belief, and because of that I kept going. Because of that I shone enough to get to the next stage, enough to be invited to Super Fours trials.

Super Fours trials were effectively England trials. Approximately eighty players from across the country were invited to attend, this number was made up of current England players and other players selected via regional training days like the ones I attended. A local club player, just a girl from Folkestone, was about to rub shoulders with the country's best, because in September 2002 I received a letter informing me that I had been selected to play in the Super Fours. My diary entry (kept intermittently for a few years but regrettably not continued) for Tuesday 3 September reads: 'Wow! Have got into super-4s. Can't quite believe it. Will be playing with England players. Oh my God. Have to go to Coventry this weekend.'

I am not sure if the 'Oh my God' was due to the fact that I would be playing alongside England players or that

I was required to go to Coventry! In my first year of trials I was placed on the same team as the then England captain Paula George, along with internationals Georgia Stevens and Susie Appleby. I could not believe that I was playing alongside these people. The structure was that we would train on a Saturday, stay overnight and play a trial match on the Sunday. I somehow managed to get through the Saturday training day without self-combusting from nerves and anxiety and progressed through to match day. I was on the red team and on the bench. My dad and Gregory came to watch the game on Sunday 8 September 2002, which was played at Broadstreet RFC in Coventry. A few minutes into the second half Paula George was subbed off. She was the current captain, she was obviously a known player, she didn't have to prove anything and she had done her job for the day. She came and stood on the side-lines about one metre away from me. This was incredible and I felt so proud, excited and inspired to be standing so close to Paula! I turned around to my dad and Gregory, who were sitting in the stand, and they could feel these emotions too. It was a proud moment and quite significant for me in my career which, considering I did not play a single second of rugby on that Sunday, speaks volumes. The following week, in the second round of trial matches, I did get on the pitch and I made a bit of an impression. That girl from Folkestone did well. Even though she was terrified and didn't think she was good enough to be there, that girl did good. I took another step up.

I did well enough to be selected for what was then the England Academy – just one step below the elite squad. The academy was coached by Gary Street assisted by

Martyn Worsley with the forwards and Ben Coombes with the backs. Although Streety excelled with England I think his real talent was in seeing potential and developing players. He was perfect for the academy and we began a player–coach relationship that developed and strengthened over the next ten years and now continues as a friendship. Although the main focus for the academy was to train and develop players, we did still play the odd fixture. The first two that I played in were against a touring America Under-23 side in January 2003, just eight months after my return from travelling. I came off the bench in the first fixture and started in the second game. In the second row, urgh, but it was still a game representing an England team. Not *the* England team, but it still felt special, as we were still wearing the rose (tulip) on our chest. We lost the first game by 7 points to nil, having found it hard to break down the defence. Streety has since given me a copy of his feedback notes after those two fixtures. These were not given out to the players at the time, but several years later, during my time as England captain, he handed them over to me after he had been sorting through some old paperwork. There were a few names that became well known and I am sure that they will not mind me sharing his comments on them, along with those about me:

Rochelle Clark – Great squad player. Fantastic attitude, Needs to get fit but very strong, works hard and has 'the dog'. Makes big tackles and has huge presence.

Tamara Taylor – Good prospect. Good ball carrier. Good hands. One for the future.

Catherine Spencer – Big, strong runner. Powerful. High in contact but promising.

Streety got his feedback spot on with both Rocky and Tamara. And with me? Well, from this first game with the academy to my sixty-third cap with England, the comments about me being too high in contact were in pretty much every piece of feedback I received. I did work hard to try to get lower over the years but not always with success! In our second game against America U23 the following week we got our revenge and beat them 18 points to 10. We were also boosted by a certain Maggie 'The Machine' Alphonsi.

Here are some extracts of Streety's notes from this game:

Rochelle Clark – Another powerful performance and definitely one for the future.

I wonder if Streety had any inkling then that Rocky would go on to become the world's most capped female rugby player, England's most capped player (male or female) and the world's most capped prop (male or female). Yep, definitely one for the future.

Tamara Taylor – Good player. Needs more experience but good hands and intelligent around the pitch.

Tamara was one of the best players I ever played alongside. She was such a skilful player and a great leader, not just in the line-out but across the rest of the pitch and throughout the squad. Her dummy in the 2014 World Cup winning final was one of the best I have seen from a second row – male or female.

Margaret Alphonsi – Influential on and off the pitch. Physical and direct. Needs to work on distribution and general handling.

Maggie did of course work on her distribution, but the change that had the most impact on what would be an incredible personal career was the switch from centre, where she played against America U23 and for her first couple of caps, to back row and to openside flanker. Geoff Richards, the England coach at the time, instigated this move and for this Maggie now owes him a pint or two!

Catherine Spencer – Excellent performance. Normally 6 but great job as second row. Strong runner – too high in contact but very promising.

I put a stop to the second-row thing, and even the blindside flanker option, at a feedback session with Streety at the end of the academy season. There was only one position I wanted to play. This debrief day was to be held at Loughborough University. The England team were going to be training there that day, so it was also a chance for us to mix a bit with the stars. How terrifying! Attendance was apparently optional, but for me it was not. I knew that I needed to go, to demonstrate my commitment. Not all of the academy squad attended that day – from memory I think there were about twelve of us. Some people are committed, others not so much.

So much of playing for England rests on actions and decisions made off the pitch, that off-pitch commitment is just as important, if not more so, than on-pitch talent. It is the combination of both that makes someone the player they will become.

I had to get up extremely early to make the journey to Loughborough. I hated these early starts but living near Folkestone in the south-east corner of the country they were all too common. My dad would often get up early too, drive the first hour for me so that I could sleep a bit more in the car, and then he would get out and get the train back to Folkestone while I continued the journey on my own. But on that day, I did the whole trip alone. I remember sitting at lunchtime in the same dining room as the England team, thinking how odd it was that physically I was so close but mentally they seemed so far away. But I could dream.

In my individual debrief with Gary Street I told him that I wanted to play number 8. I had been played at second row that season but that is not where I wanted to remain. I had already played 8 for my university and club, and my England dream, which was starting to become more vivid, featured the 8 shirt a lot.

On the way back, my journey was not so straightforward. I filled up the car with fuel soon after leaving Loughborough to avoid the exorbitant motorway prices, impressed with myself for thinking ahead. I then drove all the way to Thurrock services in Essex without stopping. It was about 11 p.m. when I stopped, tired but happy with my progress. I'd have a quick cup of tea to wake myself up, then hopefully be back home soon after midnight. I got back in the car and it would not start. My mind started racing. My dad's car, which I had borrowed for the day, was normally really reliable. I saw a man walk across the very empty and dark car park and I started having visions of him having tampered with my car and then coming to attack me! So I did what any adult would do at this point. I phoned my dad of course. He told me that there wasn't really anything he could do – I needed to phone the AA. I did so, and it wasn't until after I had logged that call that the colour of the fuel pump I had used to fill up the car many miles previously in Loughborough became clear in my mind. It was green for petrol. Not good – my dad's car was a diesel. My dad needed the car the next morning for work so I was praying that the self-proclaimed 'fourth emergency service' could help.

Whilst waiting for them to arrive I sat in the car feeling guilty about making assumptions about the man I had earlier seen walking across the car park. The recovery truck got to me just before midnight and towed the car to a garage somewhere near Dagenham where they had the facility to drain the tank. I waited in a rickety old office, on a rickety old chair, watching a fuzzy, old black-and-white TV while some poor mechanic who looked as if he had been dragged out of a deep sleep set to work. I was tired, hungry and dreaming of being in bed, snuggled up in my duvet. Eventually the car was drained. I was very grateful but at the same time also mortified at the amount I had to pay. I then headed off to find a fuel station to fill up, yet again, before heading home. A few wrong turns later (this was pre-satnav days) I eventually found my way, arriving at about 4 a.m., nearly twenty-four hours after I had left that morning – tired, much poorer, but still pleased that I had gone up to Loughborough that day.

My diary entry for the next day, 11 May 2003, reads:

Had debrief day up at Loughborough yesterday. I can't believe how quickly this rugby year has gone. Had good feedback from Gary Street. He knows my aims and I now know what I need to work on and I will. I really am going to do it this year. I want to train more, lose a stone and improve my speed off the mark and dynamism. I WILL PLAY NUMBER 8 FOR ENGLAND. It is going to take a lot of work but I am going to put my all in. A bit gutted I did not get on tour [a development tour to South Africa] but loads more happened this year than I ever dreamed of. There is always next year and a couple of World Cups!! So life is not too bad at the moment. Very skint (especially after paying £170 for the car to be drained of petrol! Don't need to remind myself of that) but just need to survive two more weeks until payday . . . Love life – pretty non-existent. Most of the time I am not too fussed but you always find yourself on the quest for Mr Right – will he be around the next corner – I hope so. I am really ready now to meet the guy that I will spend the rest of my life with. I have done the being single thing . . . Maybe I will meet someone at the gym. Can always dream!

I didn't meet the man of my dreams at the gym but I did play number 8 for England! It took me a while to find my groove though.

15 May 2003 – Feeling really down today. Not feeling too well which doesn't help but I just feel very weighted down

at the moment. I think quite a lot of the weight will be lifted when payday comes. The petrol/diesel weekend has sent me over my limit . . . even when I get paid I will still be incredibly skint . . . I also feel very fat and lardy and I can't see myself losing weight or getting any fitter. I know I will feel better when I do but I just keep snacking and stuff at the mo. I can't seem to stop myself. I came back from Loughborough with really good intentions which have now just gone to pot. I really need to get a grip . . . Hopefully next time I write in here I will be feeling more positive and happier about myself.

My next entry:

13 July 2003 — well not feeling brilliant at the moment. Have just eaten a very large curry and am feeling extremely fat.

Getting my nutrition right and eating like an elite athlete really did not come easily to me. I got much better over the years and I think in 2010 I even managed to work my way out of the 100 club — this was the name for people who recorded higher numbers on their skinfold test, or 'fat testing', as we called it. Higher numbers were not good!

At the start of the 2003–2004 season I was selected for the elite squad with my first training weekend to be held in November at Broadstreet RFC. Tamara Taylor was moved up into the elite squad that same year. Tamara was playing 8 at that point, but we were to swap positions, with Tam forging a very successful England career from the second row. I do remember Graham Smith wandering up to me that weekend and suggesting that I might like to consider moving to the front row. I can't remember what I said in reply, but I did try to avoid him as much as possible for the remainder of that season. There is no way that I would play in the front row – ever! Graham and I are now great friends. I finally forgave him.

I played just a couple of games for the England A squad during that season; one against the Nomads, where I got to play against my hero Gill Burns, and the other against Spain. The Nomads were a fifteen-a-side team made up of invited players, normally recently retired internationals or current internationals from other nations – rather like the famous invitational team the Barbarians, or the Baa-Baas as they are often known. When I played in the Nomad game I did not think about anything else other than tackling Burnsie. I made that tackle but have no recollection of the rest of the game. We played against Spain on 31 January 2004 at Imber Court in Surrey, the British Police sports ground. It was a reasonable pitch and it had a stand, but the changing rooms were about a five-minute jog from the pitch. For someone who was not overly interested in wasting energy during the warm-up this additional effort was not appreciated! In that game Maggie played on the wing (which I am sure she would have hated), Rocky was at 1, Tamara Taylor and Rachel Vickers in the second row. Sue Day was playing at 12, with Nolli Waterman and Heather Fisher on the bench. The academy and England A set-up allowed for a really good pathway for players and it was a sad day when both were relegated to the history books. I assume that this decision was driven by finance; as upset as I was at the time that the academy was disbanded, and as much as I recognised its importance for the development of players, I did appreciate that there was only a finite amount of money available for the women's game.

After these two games I was promoted from the A squad to the senior team fairly quickly. This came about as a result of an injury to another player; as is often the case in sport, one person's misfortune becomes an opportunity for another. Claire Frost had been the England number 8 for several years. She was a good, skilful player and a great character within the squad but she was starting to struggle with an ongoing Achilles tendon injury. Frosty failed a fitness test midway through the 2004 Six Nations so I was called up and was to travel with the team up to Scotland for what could be my first test. I was excited and happy at being called up but overwhelmingly nervous – that big imposter arrow was rearing its head again. I was just a girl from Folkestone; I should not be there. But someone thought I should be and I had received a letter dated 17 February 2004 informing me of the details of the upcoming weekend. We would be flying up from Heathrow so we were to meet at 8:30 a.m. and in very bold, very large letters we were told that we must bring £50 with us to contribute to the cost of the flight. Times have changed. I recorded my feelings in my diary:

19 February 2004 – In just over twelve hours I will be boarding a plane with the rest of the England squad to travel up to Scotland for the Six Nations. I have been called up to bench (Frosty injured in Spain). I may win my first cap for England in two days' time. I am trying not to dwell on this too much. I might not even play but I still can't help being

a little bit excited. I am also very nervous and scared, just being around some of the senior girls. Once more I am the new girl which is all I seem to have been doing this last year or so. I can't believe how quickly this has happened. It was only just over a year and a half ago that I went to trials to get into the regional summer training days — now I am benching for England. A few weeks ago, to add to the trend, me and five other girls from the 'A's had a photo shoot at Twickenham for *Rugby World* magazine. That was pretty awesome. The changing room was brilliant and it is highly likely that I have now sat on the same toilet as most of the present men's England squad!! Anyway, will prob write more tomorrow. Must get some sleep. Alarm is going off at 5 a.m. to get the train to Heathrow.

I love that I was so excited by the toilets! The five other players in that photo shoot were Maggie, Nolli, Amy Turner, Heather Fisher and Rocky. Whoever selected us for this feature did a pretty good job, as we all went on to enjoy successful careers.

21 February 2004 — Saturday morning, just had breakfast, twenty mins till walk and stretch. Four and a half hours till when I may win my first cap; four and a half hours till when I may just watch a game of rugby and not win my first cap. I got presented with a red rose last night which was really nice. I did have a little lump in my throat. Was quite a nice moment.

Well, it was the latter that came true. I sat and watched for eighty minutes — but I would not have described it as a game, more of an eighty-minute brawl with Karen 'Jock' Findlay at the core. She went on to forge a successful coaching career alongside a career in the police. Both of these achievements make me chuckle after my first experience of Jock!

> 9:30 p.m. – back in hotel room. I didn't get on; a bit gutted really especially due to the fact that I am missing an 'A's game tomorrow. Obviously, I can't take anything away from this and I should feel privileged to have been called up. I can't help feeling how I feel though, and that is pissed off that I didn't play. I suppose this will happen over the next couple of years, that gap between the 'A's and the main team. I can't expect to go from one team to another without having to sub. Bring on the next game!

I never played for England A again.

Twelve days after the Scotland game Geoff Richards phoned to tell me that Frosty's Achilles tendon was still causing problems. She was going to be fitness tested the following day (the day before the Wales game) and he said he would phone me after that – it was possible that I would be joining the senior team again.

The phone call came – I would be going to the Wales game. I was a little bit more confident this time, having at least met the squad, and was quite relaxed, expecting that I would not go on. Geoff did not often make tactical replacement changes in games so it was not a given than bench players would make it onto the pitch. Little did I know!

*

Sunday 21 March 2004 – Well, it has happened! Yesterday I won my first international cap for England and scored a try whilst doing so. It didn't really sink in till today. I didn't expect to get on at all in the first place, then with twenty mins left I went on. Couldn't believe it! I got a couple of good runs from the scrum and a run off the fly-half from a line-out move; then to top it off scored a cheeky little try round the blind side of a ruck. Bloody brilliant. Everyone was so nice to me afterwards and definitely made it a day to remember. Gill Burns said that it was the first day that she actually didn't mind watching and not playing. I think that was a massive compliment. I then got presented with an actual cap. I didn't realise that was going to happen so that was pretty special too. My dad has bought a bottle of port for all my coaches past and present – Woody, Jon Turbutt, O'Sullivan, McPartlin and a bottle of wine for Alan and Caddy. That is well nice of him. My mum and dad also got me a lovely paperweight from Kew Gardens that has a rose set into it. It is gorgeous. My mum and dad and Martin and Gregory are all really proud. It has been a really special weekend and one that I will never forget.

I was on such a high after my first cap. We won that game 53-3 and I thought this England thing was going to be easy. I didn't comprehend at the time how much harder things would become or quite how much my life would become dominated by the England shirt. I still remember walking into the clubhouse at Folkestone for the first time after I won that first cap. Everyone cheered; I went red and hid behind a chair. I did eventually get used to being in the limelight but it was not easy.

The following week I was selected to play number 8 against France in the final round of the Six Nations. Like England, France had won all of their games so far, so it was a winner-takes-all game. We were playing away at Bourg-en-Bresse, with the A team also travelling over to take on France A. Again, I would be heading to Heathrow with my £50 on my way to an international fixture, but this time knowing that I would be running out with the 8 shirt on my back. I was still anxious though and I still felt as though I should not be there.

Saturday 27 March 2004 – 11 a.m., kick-off 3:30 p.m. I am still not feeling nervous although I think it will soon start creeping in. Until now the actual game has been on another planet. I still can't believe it is actually going to happen. I think it is good to feel like that though. I want to save all of my nervous energy and then turn it into aggression in the game. I want to put some big tackles in today and do some good rucking, apart from my main aim of making yards with the ball. I just want to go out and have a good game. People say I have nothing to lose, I believe I have everything to lose. I have come up so quickly, I have kind of set myself a precedent. If I go out and play badly then everyone will think that it has been a mistake promoting me so quickly, I will be a bit of a one hit wonder. I really need to go out and prove myself. This is the game that counts, this is the big one.

We lost 13-12 and I don't remember much about the game itself, but I do remember that the French gave us some changing rooms a long way from the pitch, with squat toilets rather than normal toilets. Squat toilets are a challenge anyway but even more so in rugby boots with metal studs!

My next diary entry was a few weeks later:

Monday 10 May 2004 – Well, we lost the French game 13-12. I played OK but I think I could have played a lot better. Anyway, a lot has happened since then. Have just come back from Europeans and have just found out that I have been selected for the Canada Churchill Cup. Mixed emotions really. Obviously pleased to be picked but in a way would quite like a normal life for a while.

This craving for a normal life continued through my rugby career and never went away, ever. It was part of my struggle with understanding what my relationship with rugby really was, how I was meant to feel about it and what it should give me in return. But in the short term something happened which restored my desire, my ambition and motivation.

Monday 14 June 2004 – I should be in Canada at this moment but I injured my knee on tour with Folkestone a week before I was due to fly out. Absolutely gutted – a few tears were shed. I don't think I need to write it all down but the worst thing was telling Geoff that I didn't think I should go.

I already understood that the team was bigger than the individual.

I definitely made the right decision and Geoff should respect me for that but it was definitely very difficult. On the positive front it has made me realise that this England rugby lark is what I want to do. I really want to go out and have an awesome Super Four and make that 8 shirt mine. I need to get my knee fit first, have a couple of weeks off then really hit it hard. I want to be the fittest I have ever been. I also need to lost some skinfold. My diet needs to change and I want to prove to Geoff by getting under 100 skinfold that it really is what I want to do.

I don't know if I would have continued to play for England if it was not for this injury. I don't know if I would have gone on to captain my country. Missing that tour to Canada made me realise that I did not want to miss anything again. I got back to fitness and proved myself at Super Fours at the beginning of the 2004–5 season, putting in some strong performances. I went on to win my third and fourth caps against Canada who came over to England for a two-test tour. I started both games at 8. My diary entry on Christmas day 2004 summed up my change of attitude:

25 December 2004 – Sprint shuttles – hard work, pushed myself well. Need to increase reps next time.

No mention of presents, and even more surprisingly no mention of food or Christmas lunch!

In 2005 we toured New Zealand. We played the Black Ferns in two really tough fixtures, losing both, whilst also playing against and beating Samoa in a one-off fixture with them. We lost our first New Zealand test badly and I will never forget the video analysis. Geoff and Graham Smith were clearly not happy with us at all. They started the video then just walked out of the room and left us in silence. They came back in a while later and what followed was a really tough couple of hours. All of us in the room were struggling to separate our personal selves from our rugby-playing selves. As women we tend to attach too much emotion to the analysis of our performance. If we miss a tackle we think that means we are a bad person. Of course, we are not. We were much improved in the second test and played some really decent rugby. I had to play second row and jump in the line-out (not my greatest talent) as the great and influential T. J. Sutton was injured and had to fly home. Thankfully I don't think I ever again started a game in the second row for England.

In 2006 I won Player of the Year. My change in attitude was having an effect on the pitch and this in turn was helping with my self-belief struggles. Winning this award finally allowed me to accept that I was good enough to be there. The award was handed out after the last Six Nations game in 2006. We played against Ireland at Old Albanians and by beating them won the Grand Slam. We had beaten France 28-nil in France earlier in the tournament to get our revenge for two years before. *Rugby World* described our victory as 'steamrolling' the French. This was the first time I ever beat France – and I never lost to them again.

The night of the awards, we were having our post-match function in a marquee outside the main clubhouse. I remember sitting at the table not expecting to win anything and was in complete shock when my name was called. Along with a silver plate, which is still in my parents' house,

I also won a voucher for a T. M. Lewin suit and a towel. The towel was a little random but I imagine they got them for free from somewhere. I still have the T. M. Lewin suit, and I am determined that I will fit into it again one day. After the official function finished I headed straight into the clubhouse to show my award to my parents, Gregory and some of my friends. I then got drunk!

We did not drink much through the season, but when opportunities such as this arose we made up for it. I think it is important that teams are able to enjoy a night out together, and if that involves a few beers then I think that is a good thing. But after the next day we would be back to being elite athletes once more, behaving entirely 'professionally' and doing everything possible to be the best that we could be. To be fitter, faster, more knowledgeable and alongside this being positive ambassadors for our sport. Everything that we did every minute of every hour of every day was about the Rose and playing for England. We may not have been paid but we were entirely devoted to the cause. And, until the day I made the decision to retire in 2011, I too was completely and utterly, unconditionally and unquestionably, devoted to the cause.

Chapter Five
The Personality

During the autumn internationals of 2017 I become the first ever female to MC the players' post-match function at Twickenham following a men's international; something I am very proud of. Proud because I was going against the grain. People had put their faith in me. It seems mad now, but it was seen as a risk to ask a woman to do this job, but it was felt that I had the ability and credibility to deliver. It was a big thing for the council members to agree to this change, to veer away from their normal comfort zone of Martin Bayfield and the likes. It shouldn't have been, but it was a massive step.

Something I am even more proud of was being asked back for a second time, this time to MC for the men's England v Wales game during the 2018 Six Nations. This felt like a victory not just for me but also for womankind. This appointment was still reliant on individuals speaking up for the cause, in this case one of the event managers who kept pushing for a female MC until eventually the council members succumbed or agreed – whichever way you would like to interpret this!

The first time I did it the pressure was on. If I did a bad job it would be a long time before the suggestion of employing the services of a female for that role would happen again. There would also be those, I am sure, that would be happy to see me fail, confirming for them that they were right that some jobs are meant just for men. A woman doing any work in sport is responsible not just for herself but for 50 per cent of the population. We represent our gender in a different way to men, we are under the magnifying glass whether we like it or not. There are vultures, loitering with intent, waiting to pounce on any small mistake we might make to confirm their view that women can't play sport or speak in public or commentate or provide expert punditry in the studio. In contrast, when we do a good job, when we manage to deliver on stage with confidence, the patronising 'well done, you' is almost unbearable. How silly of us girls to think that we belong in this world too.

I feel completely comfortable on stage, whether as MC at Twickenham or in front of a corporate audience delivering a keynote speech or hosting an awards evening or chairing a panel, and I have always known that this job was not exclusively for the boys. It has, however, taken me a good number of years to build my profile as a speaker and it has not always been easy for me – far from it. I have not always felt so eager to stand on a stage and talk. As I developed my confidence as a rugby player, as I had to develop my confidence and skill as a captain, so too did I develop as a public speaker.

When I was in playschool I experienced my first public speaking engagement of sorts. Aged four, I was to read the nursery rhyme 'Little Bo Peep' in the end-of-year production. Gregory would be performing 'Baa Baa Black Sheep'. I had a nice pink dress, and really looked the part as I headed up to the stage. My mum was in the audience and my brother was to the side of the stage waiting for his turn in the limelight. I had rehearsed at home and I knew all of the words, so what could possibly go wrong? Well, nothing much went right. I stood for a few seconds before commencing my oration – timing is everything. I opened my mouth to deliver the first line and instead of the appropriate words coming out of my mouth, a howling wail burst forth. The whole experience was just far too much for me and I stood crying on the stage for what felt like minutes, though it was probably just a few seconds, before I ran down from the stage and found my mum. I remember then snuggling into the comfort of her lap to watch the incredible recital of 'Baa Baa Black Sheep' by Gregory Spencer.

The thing about performances not going well though is that it is commonplace for a chance to come along sooner or later to put things right – a bit like sport. To make amends and get back on track. This opportunity came a couple of years later when we were in infants' school, as Gregory and I were again to be involved in the big school production, *Peter and the Wolf*. My brother, who it was clear had a talent for acting, was given the lead role of Peter – albeit because the original Peter had chicken pox and had to step down, but Gregory played the part with great aplomb. If Gregory was Peter, I hear you ask, what part did I play? There are plenty of other starring roles in *Peter and the Wolf* – the wolf for one, also the duck, the cat and the bird, but I, Catherine Spencer, played the part of a tree. Trees neither move a great deal nor do they speak. The casting directors had obviously watched my previous performance and felt that I could not be trusted to do anything else. I was fairly tall which was really the only talent required. That and standing still. My parents came to watch and I am sure were equally proud of both of us, but my stage presence and confidence were suffering from a slow start.

Move on several years and unbelievably in secondary school I took GCSE drama. This option was slightly unexpected, and in truth was because I did not want to do art and the way the subject choices were grouped I had to do one of them. Of the two I was worse at art – I was really, really, really bad at art. So drama it was . . . and what a great choice it turned out to be. Without making any comments or judgements about the quality of the teaching staff, the reality was that everyone got a B for GSCE drama unless you were actually good in which case you got an A. On our assessment day we had to perform a play in which I was an army officer who was organising some kind of celebration event. This was great news for me because I had a clipboard as a prop, which had the added benefit of making it extremely easy for me to place my script on the clipboard and read the whole thing from start to finish. No words had to be learned. No real acting had taken place, but somehow I ended up with a B in GCSE drama.

For some reason, always wanting to challenge myself, I then decided to enter the senior school Shakespeare competition. I hated Shakespeare at school so why was I doing this? I did not have a good track record in learning words or acting. About a third of the way through my monologue (which I think was from *Othello*) I completely forgot my words. Ever prepared, I had placed one of my friends in the stage wings to prompt me, but I was struggling to hear her. What followed next was an excruciating five minutes of me, centre stage and before a sizeable audience, asking my prompter what the next line was, not hearing so asking again, not hearing again so asking again, eventually hearing the line, delivering the line then repeating the same cringeworthy process with each new line. After five minutes reality hit me and I decided that I no longer should be on that stage and I walked off, much to the relief of all involved. But, despite this, I still had the feeling that I wanted to be on a stage, that I wanted my voice to be heard.

Undaunted I attempted acting just one more time, in a leading role with a local amateur dramatics society. They needed a teenage girl in their upcoming production and they could not find any other willing volunteers in my home town, a town of nearly 15,000 people. I found it hard to say that very simple word 'no' (a trend that continued for many years) and I felt bad that they could not find anyone, so I put my hand up and said yes. There were hours and hours of rehearsals. I did manage to learn my lines this time but my delivery can only really be described as monotonous. I tried desperately hard to act but my performance did not match the effort, a bit like my ability to sidestep on the rugby pitch – highly adept and skilful in my mind but the execution not quite matching up! It had taken me all this time, from my first attempt at playschool to this starring role in amateur dramatics, to realise that although I was comfortable on stage, in front of an audience, thespian I was not. Acting really was not my thing, and once I let go of that and found ways to tell my own story or promote my sport I never looked back. So when media work, and particularly public speaking, became real possibilities in my sporting career, I sought opportunities, developed confidence, honed my talent and constantly worked to improve. It has become something that I enjoy, am good at and relish. But as always it didn't start easily.

It was about 8:30 a.m. on a weekday morning, shortly after I won my first cap in 2004. I had requested a late start at my job because I had a 'big' media gig: a live telephone interview with Radio Kent. I had never done a live interview before and to say that I was nervous is an understatement. I was living with my parents at the time and spoke to the radio show from the phone in our back room in Hythe, a world away from international rugby. Fifteen years on, talking on the radio is fairly commonplace for me and nerves do not come into the equation, but that first time was different. Some people become confident through experience and I fall into the category: no experience equals zero confidence. But I got through that first interview, and then I did another and another and another and I loved it!

I now relish the buzz of media, especially live media, and the more challenging the question the better. As an England rugby player, I was getting some media requests but when I became England captain this stepped up to a new level. Being exposed to media was one of the things that I enjoyed most about the captaincy and was an area of the leadership task that I felt truly confident with. I knew that I was good at it. My mum was in the house when I did that first live radio interview and she also recalls how big that moment felt. How times change – roll on a few years and I was delivering live commentary to an audience of over two million on prime-time Saturday-evening TV with ITV. I still make appearances on Radio Kent too, who have been loyal in their support and promotion of me since the early days.

At the 2006 World Cup media requests started to ramp up; I remember doing a live Radio 4 *Today* programme interview from a hotel room in Canada. One of the questions that they asked me was when would women be good enough to play against the men? This was not asked in a challenging way but more of a patronising 'well done for being a girl and playing sport but when are you going to actually be good enough to play properly' way. Internally raging but being very diplomatic and the good ambassador that I was for England rugby, I provided a polite, assured and insightful answer. But, this question and similar ones in other interviews just kept up a continuous drip feed of the opinion that as women we were second-class citizens as far as our sport was concerned. We were not as good as men and never would be. We did not have as much value and silly us for thinking that we ever would do.

One of the jobs of a Six Nations captain is to attend the annual launch, so I was there in that role in 2008, 2009 and 2010. In 2008 I think I gave four interviews. My male counterpart would have been giving ten times that, probably more. In 2009 there was a development of sorts in that all of the women's captains were allotted a set time to appear in the main press room, but a major flaw in this plan was that the organisers failed to communicate this on the schedule to any of the journalists in attendance or market this fact to any media outlets. Our time in the press room also conflicted with the men's press opportunities and the media turnout was poor. Again, not surprising at the time, but yet another dent in our confidence, another voice in our heads telling us that we were not worth anything, we didn't have any value, that we were an inconvenience. Things did start to improve and in 2010 I think I reached double figures for interviews, but this was without doubt down to the incredible hard work and determination of our media manager, Julia Hutton. Not the RFU, not the Six Nations, but one individual. Thanks to my position as captain I saw up close the work that Julia was doing; she got little support but despite this achieved so much at the time to build media relations on behalf of England Women.

This dependence upon the actions of one, motivated individual is true of so many levels of women's rugby, whether it is setting up a new girls' team or running the women's section for a club. At elite level, whether it is pushing and running the England women's game or driving media, the success of this is still down to one or two key people. Building effective relationships within and outside the RFU is crucial – it is therefore vitally important that we have the right individuals in the right jobs. At the time of writing I don't think that we have the right people leading our game, so I really hope that things change.

In 2007 one of my first tasks as England captain was to attend the Sports Personality of the Year awards. It was the first time that anyone from women's rugby had been invited, so along I went with Gary Street. Streety was shown to his seat somewhere near the back and I was directed towards the front. I thought that there must have been some kind of mistake. I was sitting immediately behind Tim Henman and returning winner Zara Phillips. What was I doing there? For the first time ever, I seemed to have been placed on something approaching a level playing field. It was not all a positive experience though. The worst part was that the powers-that-be in women's rugby had insisted that I wear the formal England suit that we were required to wear after matches. Not a nice dress or skirt but my ill-fitting, unflattering trouser suit. Thank you very much. How to make me feel drab and unfeminine in one quick step – on television, surrounded by amazing sports people. But it was good to be there. Fast-forward seven years and at least the team were dressed appropriately when they picked up their Team of the Year awards. Nothing to do with the powers-that-be but, I understand, the result of player power and influence. Well done to Nolli Waterman for arranging a clothing sponsor for the occasion.

When I became captain this also meant that on a couple of occasions I was allowed into the sacred, very male world of the England training home at Pennyhill Park. One day Steve Borthwick (the men's captain at the time) and I did a few joint interviews, a big one for *Rugby World* along with some women's 2010 World Cup build-up promotion. I mainly remember being worried about the extortionate cost of the toasted panini I was chomping my way through whilst waiting for Steve. The polar opposite worlds of men's rugby and women's rugby symbolised very aptly by a couple of pieces of toast, some filling, a posh name and a salad garnish. I had already had to pay for my petrol to get to Pennyhill Park and was running low, but Julia Hutton could see my worry, came to my rescue and bought my panini for me on that day. Thank you, Jules!

Starting to become a 'personality' is not limited to newspapers, radio, TV and distant audiences. It can be more intimate and more embarrassing and awkward to deal with until it starts to feel more normal and eventually right. The first few times I was asked for my autograph I used to shy away because I was worried that they were not asking me but someone behind me or one of the men or someone 'proper'. Why on earth would someone want my autograph? But people kept asking and not all of these people could be wrong, could they? Over time, with every signature that I wrote, it began to feel more comfortable and I started to accept that, yes, people did want the autograph of Catherine Spencer, to the extent that along with my phone, wallet, keys and mascara, a Sharpie was frequently on my 'don't forget to pack' list.

It was important how I reacted to such requests too; shying away and questioning why they would want the autograph of a female rugby player was not helpful to me or the sport and was disappointing to that person. I was devaluing myself, and women's rugby along with it, but I didn't realise that at the time. In 2009 I was asked for an autograph in real life. By that I mean not in a rugby or sport setting. I was back home for Christmas and travelling into Canterbury to do some shopping with my mum. We were on the park-and-ride bus when someone asked me for my autograph. I could not believe it! I was not in England stash (I never wore it unless on England duty), I was not in rugby kit, I was not even in sportswear. I was in normal clothes that any thirty-year-old woman might wear to go Christmas shopping and still I was recognised. I felt pretty good about that, and gladly and confidently gave my autograph.

One of the more traumatic media experiences of my time with England was appearing on an episode of the well-known TV quiz show *Eggheads* in 2006. It was decided that it would be great profile to send five members of the squad onto the show. So Sue Day, Tamara Taylor, Sophie Hemming, Maggie Alphonsi and I found ourselves there. Unfortunately, our secret weapon, Katie Storie, who was the brains of the squad, was ill and could not make it. We all had to attend an audition day to make sure that we could chat well enough around our answers rather than just simply replying 'I don't know' – even if that was generally the case! Somehow, even after the audition, they still thought it was a sensible idea to proceed, so our filming date at the BBC studios in London was set. I drove to Shepherd's Bush in my little red Micra and managed to find the BBC – first challenge completed. I then managed to find the car park and find a space but that is where my luck ran out.

I was running late by this point due to awful traffic, so my stress levels were already a little bit high. Then I couldn't find any way to get out of the car park and into the studio. I could not find an exit door anywhere. Not one without a big sign attached warning that alarms would go off if opened. I must have spent a good twenty minutes walking round and round trying to escape. Eventually I made the decision to risk an alarmed fire exit, thinking to myself that surely the doors wouldn't *actually* be alarmed; the signs were probably just advisory. Boy, was I wrong. I pushed the door a millimetre and the noise was deafening. I was rooted to the spot. About ten seconds later a scary-looking security guard turned up and asked me what on earth I was doing. I explained I was trying to get to the studio to take part in a quiz show but that I could not work out how to get out of the car park. He said two words: 'Turn around.' Oh my goodness, was I getting arrested?! I did as I was told and saw straight ahead of me a large sign that said 'pedestrian exit'. I don't know how I had missed it.

The show itself did not go much better. I did actually manage to get two questions right but overall none of us managed to get enough questions correct to get through our round, which meant that Sue Day was left to fight the final round on her own. Let's just say, we were better rugby players than we were quizzers. The worst thing about this was that I then allowed myself to go through this trauma again, appearing on a celebrity episode in 2017. Maggie was on that show too, along with Goldie Sayers (javelin), Ebony Rainford-Brent (cricket) and Sarah Stevenson (tae kwon do). I only answered one question correctly. I won't be attempting a third appearance. It was interesting to compare the shows though. In 2006 I had the feeling that we shouldn't really have been there, we didn't get paid and if I remember correctly we had to fund our own travel costs both to the audition and to the filming day. In 2017 in stark contrast I did think we should be there as part of a celebrity series and that time, quite rightly, we did get paid and our travel was organised for us along with a paid-for hotel room in Glasgow where it was filmed. I even thought that our team were worthier of the celebrity tag than the team that followed us. Things really had changed!

In 2010, prior to the World Cup, a launch event was held at City Hall on the banks of the River Thames. The organisers got this spot on; it was a great setting and worthy of our value. All the team captains were bussed there from our training base at Surrey Sports Park, along with a coach and various managers or media managers. As the host captain my day was a little busier than others, culminating in me delivering an off-the-cuff speech following a question-and-answer session hosted by Alex Payne, of Sky Sports fame, on stage in front of many journalists and dignitaries. It felt easy, I enjoyed it and didn't think much of it, but when I came off stage a lot of people made the effort to speak to me and tell me what a great job I had done. Looking back now I guess that I did. Little Bo Peep was nowhere to be seen! So I continued fulfilling media requests with relish for the remainder of my England career, whether it was on the radio, on TV, for a newspaper or providing my own quotes for internal RFU press releases organised by Julia. My own media impact grew more after retirement but again it didn't always feel like that. There were still many occasions when I was hit back down, reminded that I was only a woman, just that girl from Folkestone. I had to continually remind myself that I was valuable. I had to cling on to my confidence hard sometimes, for fear that it would be lost from my grasp completely.

My 'sandwich girl' moment, as I call it, came during the 2015 Six Nations when I was commentating at Twickenham for a women's international game that was taking place immediately after the men's fixture. At Twickenham there is a small press room where journalists and commentators can assemble, chat to each other and grab a sandwich or two and a tea or coffee. I was in the press room when I was asked by a male journalist if I could get some more sandwiches. His assumption that I was there for no other reason than to re-stock sandwiches and top up drinks unfortunately did not surprise me. I passed the gentleman a platter of sandwiches, and then proceeded to have a very loud conversation, within his earshot, about my England captaincy with a journalist whom I did know, and the look on that man's face was priceless. A few years later, in another food-related incident, I was taking part in a 'scrum dine with me' challenge for Wooden Spoon, the children's charity of rugby, along with Rob Henderson (Ireland and Lions), Ollie Phillips (Rugby Sevens) and John Taylor (Lions legend, famous commentator, etc.). One of the celebrity judges, who shall remain nameless but has gained fame through one of the more popular culinary TV shows and loved a buttery biscuit base, did not acknowledge me when I was first introduced, by John, whom I was chatting to at the time, as Catherine. He thought I was just a girl. I was, he got that right, but it was not until I donned my chef's whites that he realised I was one of the rugby celebrities. He did then have the grace to apologise, but again, thank you for making me feel small, for denting my confidence and reminding me that the big imposter arrow was still dangling above my head.

I have done a lot of commentating since retiring and I hope to do more, but it took a few years of persuasion from Julia before I ventured towards it. Before that I had always said no to commentary requests. I was enjoying being in the studio. In the studio it is warm, there are tea and food supplies and it is pretty easy too. You get to watch the game and have forty minutes to think about what you might say at half-time and then again after the game. And even then, depending on the structure of the broadcast, you may only speak for a few minutes. To be honest it is easy money, and along with getting fed you also get your make-up and hair done, which I always enjoy. On commentary you are required to concentrate and think clearly the whole time and you get none of the associated benefits of being in the studio. Whenever I watched rugby with my family or friends I always missed things, my mind always wandered, so I was really worried that this might happen during commentary, but finally I said yes.

My first commentary gig was about as no-frills as it could get, but this was good because it meant if I was awful not too many people would hear! I was to commentate for the RFU live stream alongside Nick Heath at a Six Nations match at Esher Rugby Club. I can't remember which game it was, but what I can remember is that it was freezing cold. My dad brought me hot tea midway through and I was so grateful! I don't recall being particularly good but I do remember thinking that I was not terrible. I was good enough to give myself that little bit of confidence required to do it again, and again and then again. Now I would rather be on commentary than in the studio. I get to talk more for one thing! I don't get my make-up done or sit in the warm but that is OK; there are other opportunities for that.

I have also written a lot more in retirement and have had articles published for various outlets including the *Sunday Times*, *Independent on Sunday* and the *Guardian* as well as regular columns in the *Rugby Paper* enjoying various moments of tit for tat with Jeff Probyn (someone has to!). I enjoy writing, as it gives me the opportunity to put some real thought into my message. The first article I wrote with significant clout was in 2015. I wrote a 'one year on' article for the *Sunday Times* following the 2014 World Cup. England Women had won and were on top of the world, but one year later it was clear that things had come crashing down. Looking back at the article now it seems quite subtle and fair and highlights an area of the game that the RFU now seems to be in agreement with, judging by their actions.

The article was headlined WOMEN'S RUGBY LOSES WAY AFTER WORLD CUP WIN. I highlighted the swinging pendulum of focus for women's rugby at the time. Our World Champions became only the second female sports team to win Team of the Year at the BBC Sports Personality of the Year awards in fifty-two years. This was huge. What an incredible opportunity to seize the moment, to attract sponsors to the game and finally reap some rewards for years and years of hard work, blood, sweat and tears on and off the pitch for all involved in women's rugby. An incredible opportunity, yes, but not one that was taken up. Quite the opposite. The fifteen-a-side game was decimated, attention turned to Sevens and for our Red Roses, with so many key players removed from club and country, Gary Street removed and Graham Smith following suit; the result was their worst Six Nations result ever. I was embarrassed watching some of the games and the performance in front of me. An expectant new audience had been let down and lots of hard work by many people was shattered by the decisions made that year.

From a personal perspective my credibility as a commentator on the women's game was upheld. At the same time my relationship with some people at the RFU became strained. Not long after the article was published I was due to a be a judge for the National Rugby Awards. I was looking forward to it, and as someone who had been involved in the sport at every level I was well qualified. The awards were run by the *Rugby Paper* but significantly partly funded by the RFU. Shortly before the awards ceremony I got an unexpected email from the *Rugby Paper* telling me they had been informed that I was not able to be a judge any more. The RFU (or some individuals there) had requested that I be removed from the judging list.

A former England captain who had worked tirelessly for years promoting the sport, I had been blacklisted for sharing in that article in the *Sunday Times* what everyone could see. Again, I was treated differently because of my gender; there are countless opinion articles written by male former rugby players. But this was new for women's rugby, and my article was seen as negative, not as the positive it should have been in that the media were taking note and printing wider opinions about our game. Eventually, after lots of back and forth and support from various influencers including Sue Day, my position as judge was reinstated. Quite a ridiculous situation, but it did not overly surprise me. Since that time, with new personnel joining the RFU, my relationship with them has improved, but I will continue to advocate for the development of our sport even if my view does not always toe the party line.

I am happy to use my profile and influence. I have become something of a go-to person for comment on any slightly controversial topic regarding women's rugby. Most current or former players will not talk, but I am a free agent. In 2018 a BBC article that featured my comments headlined the BBC sports webpage for quite some time. The headline this time was LACK OF LEADERSHIP and an associated column in the *Rugby Paper* was given a full-page spread. Sometimes I want to walk away from all this, escape somewhere with my husband and not read any rugby media – but for the time being something drives me on. I enjoy writing and media work so why not use rugby as my platform? I am not actively seeking out media opportunities – partly because I don't want to feel let down when the doors do not open for me, but also because there are other things in my life that require time and attention – yet if I am presented with them I will take them. And if I get paid, then even better. I was never paid to play rugby for club or country so I do not feel guilty for receiving financial reward (albeit relatively small) for associated work now.

A couple of years ago I enjoyed one of the more surreal afternoons of my life when I was awarded an Honorary Doctorate from Canterbury Christ Church University. Walking down the aisle of the impressive Canterbury Cathedral as part of the formal procession of dignitaries, dressed to the nines in formal gowns and hats in front of hundreds of former students waiting to collect their degree certificates and a huge throng of excited and proud parents, was not normal. The national anthem was played to begin proceedings and brought back memories of being in shorts and socks rolled down to my ankles. I gave the same bow of my head though, the same nod to my parents whilst other people around me chose to sing. After standing and listening to the oration describing my career through rugby and beyond I was offered the chance to speak. These were my words:

I am receiving this on behalf of all those I have played alongside and all those whom I have played against. Those who have gone before me and those who continue to shape and develop the game.

It is for everyone who is striving for equality of opportunity here in the UK and abroad. It is for the volunteers I am currently working with in Zimbabwe and for friends in Uganda, Zambia and Kenya who are all continuing to inspire.

For those of you collecting your degrees today, congratulations and enjoy your graduation evening celebrations – I have no doubt you will. Do not be afraid to seek out or grasp opportunities that may take you towards a road less travelled. Look up and look around; always look forward because that path less travelled often brings with it the greatest reward.

I would also like to take this opportunity to thank my parents, who are here. If any parents here or future parents want some advice on achieving the perfect balance between encouraging but not pushing, then speak to my parents because they are the experts. To my husband, who is also here, thank you for helping me to look forward again and embarking on my own new road less travelled.

And lastly and perhaps unusually I am going to state that I am receiving this on behalf of myself. I am always telling others that it is important to value ourselves and to recognise our own achievements so today I am going to practise what I preach. Thank you.

The last sentence is the most significant for me and marks a development in the way I think about myself, and about how we should all think about ourselves. It marks the occasion, nearly fifteen years after I won my first cap, seven years after I retired, when I finally, truly accepted myself as the personality.

Chapter Six
The Little Red Car

Being an international athlete does not finish at the final whistle of a match, nor does it finish when we hear the sounds of the gym door closing behind us as we go home or go to our day job. Being an international athlete of any kind is full-time. In fact, it is more than full-time: it is life. It becomes us, every moment of every day, probably more so when we are not paid, when we do not receive a salary and match fees. Why? Because our motivation goes beyond money. We are driven by something all-encompassing. We have a passion, but we also feel as if we have an obligation or higher calling to contribute to the development of the game. To spread the word.

I made what felt like hundreds of player appearances throughout and beyond my playing career. I attended rugby clubs and schools and charity events in my capacity as England captain, most of which I drove myself to. Before I started working for the RFU and I was given a company car, I used to drive a little red Nissan Micra – for those of you of the younger variety (i.e. not as old as me) look up a Nissan Micra W-reg and see what comes up. That is what

I drove – I loved it but was also embarrassed by it. It's a car associated with grannies – certainly not international athletes. Sometimes kids would see me drive into the school or club and I am sure I could see disappointment on their faces. I was asked on more than one occasion, when I had not already been spotted in my car, if I drove a convertible. I was also asked even more often if I was rich. I used to give a very diplomatic answer about money not being the reason for me playing, focusing on what I did get out of playing rugby for my country rather than letting them know that no, I was far from rich, that I was working as an office manager in a less than £16K per year job, or that during the 2010 World Cup I was officially unemployed.

When the kids were disappointed at seeing my car it was not because they particularly equated England captaincy with posh sports cars; rather it was because they associated sports captaincy with being cool and exciting and living a celebrity life. I hated disappointing them so I tried my hardest not to. At one rugby club visit a young boy who must have only been about eight or nine asked me if I had met Justin Bieber. It just so happened that I had been to Madame Tussaud's the day before, discussing the possibility of holding a Tag Rugby Trust charity event there. Justin had been replicated in wax there, so I was able to say to that boy that yes, I had met Justin Bieber. I think this was OK! But generally these player appearances were great and I still love giving school assemblies. When I receive a message from a teacher or parent saying that one of the kids has started playing a sport because of my talk, it feels wonderful. It inspires me to keep going, to keep spreading the word. I am not asking them to dream of being a World

Champion or Olympic gold medallist, I am simply asking them to look up and look forward and to take their next step, whatever that might be. As a young girl I didn't know where I would eventually end up but I always had some idea of what my next step would be; I also knew that rugby would play a big part.

I was always going to play rugby; I just happen to have been born female. Things would have been different, however, had I enjoyed the same career as a male. Home World Cup final captain, two-time World Cup finalist, six-time Six Nations winner, England Player of the Year . . . I could go on. What on earth would my life be like had I been born male? Well, I wouldn't be competing for the tiny fraction of media work offered to us females to start with. For our male counterparts, upon retirement media doors are often thrown open, but I had to work to seek out the doors, negotiate my own way towards these doors and try to make enough noise that they would be opened. Sometimes they creaked open, other times they were left firmly shut. I was told by one major media company that I would not get much more work from them because I did not win a World Cup. I don't think this made me any less capable of doing my job as studio pundit or commentator so the decision hurt on that level, but what stung even more was that this rule was not applied to the men.

As a male player I would have been rewarded well financially for playing for club and country and I certainly would not be complaining about playing too much rugby, as some male professionals are doing now. Count your lucky stars. There are so many people crying out to be where you are and to have your job – although, to some extent surprisingly, I am not one of them. I am glad I was not paid to play for my country. Times have changed and I fully support the move towards professional women's rugby for reasons of equality, but I don't actually think that anyone should be paid to play for their country. I understand that a lot of money is made, and the players are at the centre of it, but I don't think there are many rugby players out there that would begrudge that money going back into the grassroots game – or I should re-phrase: I *hope* there are not many rugby players out there who would begrudge that. Their agents may think differently of course! Yes, get paid by your clubs, earn your bread and butter that way if you are in a position to do so (women's rugby is getting closer to that ideal and the RFU central contracts are essential until the clubs can become the employer), get paid for extra work you may do to help promote and develop the game or for sponsorship work gained off the back of being an international player, but play for your country for other reasons. For pride, for yourself, your family, your friends, your community and your country. Not everything has to be driven by money. Understand the privilege and let performance be driven by something other than a pay cheque.

Money is not always the answer, as we have seen in various football World Cups and men's rugby World Cups. The best performances and successes are driven by and sustained effectively by a strong sense of internal motivation. Money might spark this, but it does not keep it burning. It should not be the biggest motivator. The Irish women's hockey team famously won a silver medal at the 2018 Hockey World Cup against all odds. Many members of the team were self-funded, in stark contrast to most other teams in the tournament, which shows what can happen if you are motivated in the right way. If I had been paid to play rugby, if that is all I ever did, I would not feel so credible delivering talks and working as a public speaker. I can talk with credibility and from the heart about working hard and pushing to get to the next stage. I did that: 100 per cent me and my motivation.

When I first got into the England set-up I was working as a police caseworker processing the admin surrounding road-traffic incidents. It was my job to compile files following incidents ranging from small bumps and dented wing mirrors to, at the other end of the scale, fatalities. It was not the most glamorous job but I enjoyed criminology; my dad was a probation officer, and I think that if rugby had not taken over I would have pursued a career somewhere in the criminal justice system. When I won my first cap I was still working at Kent Police. Heading back into work the following Monday morning brought me down to earth quite significantly. When I left the office early on the afternoon of Friday 4 March 2004 to travel up to the team hotel before the Wales game the next day, following a late call-up, no one at work had any idea where I was going. Unusually for me I had built up enough flexitime to not take leave, so I didn't need to tell them. I just packed up my stuff and walked out to my car, not quite knowing what to think. The next day and winning my first cap would change my life. Working for the police also entitled me to be selected for the British Police team. I played a number of games for them during my time with Kent Police but this was not easy. I had to negotiate to get any time off and the majority of the time I did take was part of my annual leave entitlement or unpaid leave. I think I got two days' special sports leave in total, which at the time I felt incredibly grateful for.

In 2005 I moved to Bristol. I was finally ready to leave my beloved Folkestone Ladies' team and start my premiership rugby journey. I didn't want to play for a London club (urgh!) and I had friends living in Bristol so it was the natural choice. My dad was over the moon as it meant he had a reason to visit his native West Country more often! The first job I picked up was a six-month contract working for VOSA (the Vehicle and Operator Services Agency) processing vehicle operator licences. Joy of joys. The relief when I heard that they were cutting back jobs and that my contract would not be renewed was very evident. Apart from the incredibly boring nature of the job itself I felt a little out of my comfort zone. The person I sat opposite was, by her own description, an 'extreme knitter'. For those of you who don't know what this means, neither did I, but she showed me photos – she would be hung up by big meat hooks and knit. Don't ask. I had to get out of there.

After trawling through newspaper job sections (times have changed!) I saw an advert for the position of office manager working at a sports centre near Bristol. I did not have a huge amount of experience but I had worked on reception at a gym in a hotel for a year before I went travelling, so I kind of bigged that up a bit and got the job. I started at Yate Leisure Centre, part of South Gloucestershire Leisure Trust at the time, in March 2006. Just four weeks after starting I slightly apprehensively strolled into my manager's office and requested two months off work so that I could go to the 2006 World Cup. My boss asked me if I would quit if I didn't get the time off to which, with no hesitation, I replied that yes, I would. She gave me the time off but in return she got four years of hard work out of me.

I really enjoyed my time there. I had to learn everything on the job because, honestly, I had no idea what I was doing, but it was great. When I got there the office was in a complete mess. There were no processes or systems and pricing was seemingly plucked out of the air. The office had been run by the same two people for twenty-five years on a job-share basis. Then I came in and changed pretty much everything. I guess looking back I was showing a lot of leadership – whether I was getting the confidence from my rugby or it was the other way around I don't know. I rolled out order processing systems, became apt at financial reconciliations, started reporting weekly and monthly centre activity and so on. This just did not exist before I was there. So when I came to negotiate flexible and reduced hours running up to 2010, they were granted. As were the ten additional days' leave that I used my influencing skills to add into the HR policy for sportspeople. The job could be frustrating at times, and some of the customers I occasionally had to deal with were downright rude, but generally I really enjoyed it and got on well with my colleagues.

Importantly, I could also forget about the job as soon as I walked out of the door and focus on my other 'job' – playing for England. Equally when I walked in the door on a Monday morning I could switch off from England rugby – just as vital for my sanity. The experience I gained in that job has also helped me with the running of my own business. Being a female international rugby player requires an individual not just to be good at their sport, not just to be determined and motivated and mentally fit, but also to be a good mediator and negotiator. Managing the work/rugby balance was a massive part of being a female England rugby player. It was a challenge, but I found that I seemed to be good at it, building long-term relationships and negotiating with employers and colleagues. This has stuck with me and again has set me in good stead for the development of my own business and building my own profile. I would not have learned and developed these skills if I had been a professional and full-time rugby player.

Although having a job when I was playing was a good thing for a number of reasons – it paid the bills, taught me skills and provided a release – there were times during my rugby career when work had to take second place. Rugby was without doubt my priority. There was not always the time emotionally or physically for work *and* rugby.

Six months prior to the 2010 World Cup I negotiated with my employers to allow me to continue to deliver my job within reduced hours; as part of a wider restructure I then reduced my hours even further a couple of months later, which allowed me more time to focus on the build-up to the World Cup. I never got paid to play but at this time we could access loss of earnings from the RFUW and this allowed me to top up the balance of reducing to part-time work as well as helping a little during the tournament itself. As we got closer to the tournament my thoughts started to turn towards leaving work completely. It would be tough financially but all I was working towards was lifting that World Cup trophy with the team. I didn't want any distraction or other focus during the tournament so I made the decision to hand in my notice. It felt like the right thing to do at the time but now I can say with some certainty that it was the wrong decision. My selfish dream of winning the World Cup was impacting on my life once more. I didn't have another job to move to when I made the decision to quit. I delivered my resignation letter and thought that if all else failed I could sell my flat and move back in with my parents. I hadn't asked my parents, but I am sure that they would have been fine about it! Looking back, what I should have done was ask for a career break, as I did in 2006, and stay on to develop and move up in the leisure industry. I would be better off financially now if I had made the more sensible decision back then. Nor would I have had to endure four years working for the RFU. There are lots of people who have worked for the RFU for many years and loved it. But for me, rugby player through and through, passionate about the game and developing opportunities for others, rather surprisingly the fit was not right.

After I left my office manager post and during the build-up to the World Cup, whilst we were in and out of training camps I happened to see a vacancy for the role of south-west women's rugby development manager. I lived in Bristol, I loved rugby, I needed a job after the World Cup – this seemed to be a sign. So I applied. The RFUW obviously knew me well, but I had to apply and interview for the role anyway. The timing of the interview was not ideal. At all. One of our squad training camps was held in the Brecon Beacons with the army. Three days of team-building, character-building, forced sleep deprivation – why in the build-up to a World Cup anyone thought that sleep deprivation was a good idea I have no idea but someone obviously did. Because that is what you do. You go on these military-based team-building camps and apparently it gives you a better chance of winning the World Cup. Well, it didn't work for us. We finished there on the Wednesday afternoon and at 9 a.m. on Thursday morning in Twickenham I had my job interview. I had to drive down to London on the Wednesday afternoon, which was highly dangerous after two nights of no sleep out in the woods. It was hardly an ideal situation for the team captain, in the lead-up to the home World Cup. I did somehow manage to drive to London without falling asleep and crashing. I also somehow managed to get through the interview without falling asleep and then managed to get myself the job. I negotiated an October start so I had got that minor annoyance out of the way – job sorted. Now all my focus and energy could go on the World Cup – and catching up on sleep.

All through my rugby career I was financially poor, and I continued to get poorer post-retirement. From 2014 to the end of 2016 after I retired I experienced two of my toughest years financially, when I made the decision to leave the RFU and set up my own company. These were times of huge stress and almost certainly periods of associated depression. Having to ask people to lend me money was starting to become a necessity. Not knowing how I was going to pay the mortgage next month was pretty stressful and I felt ashamed. I couldn't let people see that I was struggling financially. I was former England captain – how could that be? I was strong.

Part of the problem was that I was still giving my time up too cheaply, often for free. I was not recognising my own value, and I was certainly not practising what I was preaching at the time. But there were a lot of lessons learned during that two-year period. I started to build up a good business network and I am certain that the successes I see now are due to the hard work for little return back then, but in the process I nearly drove myself to ruin. There were so many times when I sat, alone in my house, on the bottom step of the stairs with my head in my hands, crying. A speaking engagement that someone had cancelled or Maggie getting a media job rather than me meant huge worry and financial stress for me. I felt that I was all too often paving the way for others to reap the rewards and I was finding that really tough.

My first paid media gig was for the BBC. I appeared on *Woman's Hour* and received £58. I was so excited on both fronts but I would have gone on *Woman's Hour* for free, no doubt about that. I am not sure if the £58 even covered my travel expenses but I still remember receiving that cheque and it made me feel valued. More recently I declined a commentating job for the BBC because it did not pay enough. I have also recently turned down a potentially exciting media project with a private commercial media outlet because I can't justify my time against the fee offered. This is not entirely a reflection on the fees, but it *is* a reflection on how I now value myself differently.

I may still be paving the way for others; it may be that individuals like me turning down work means others like me will be paid what they deserve. This is a good thing but am not going to pretend that this is not wholly frustrating for me. My husband, Jeremy, always tells me that I am ten years too early and I agree to some extent. But then I would not have been able to make the same impact that I believe I am making now. I may be losing out on money and making life difficult for myself, but I have a value. I am constantly telling other sportswomen and former rugby players that they have a value. I now have to practise what I preach and learn from that tough time after 2014. Now that I am running my own company I have come to understand the value of time and more specifically the value of *my* time, but that knowledge has been gained by my sheer determination to get through the hard times, to ignore the situations that implied that we women were not as important as the men. That we had very little value. It was not easy to get through this, and of course I still come up against such situations, but I now know how and when to say no.

Recently I attended a black-tie rugby event with Maggie and Rocky. Not a bad line-up. During the evening several current and former male internationals were invited up to the stage to take part in question-and-answer sessions hosted by, of course, Martin Bayfield. Maggie did get to go on stage to deliver the toast to the Queen (apparently that was required) and got to say a couple of words about the development of the girls' game (a highly unoriginal question) and later in the evening I got my chance to go on stage too. But I did not get to say anything, not a single word. My job was to draw the raffle and to smile sweetly (someone actually told me to do that). This was unacceptable and degrading, but a few years ago I would have been pleased that I was asked to go on stage at all.

Many years ago I was invited to attend the annual Rugby Players' Association (RPA) dinner. I remember feeling grateful to have been asked. I was sitting at a table with a couple of the other England players right at the back of the room; out of the way, but a little tick in the box for the organisers that there were at least a couple of token female players in the room. I have been to many dinners and events over the years and it has taken time to start to be recognised. Event hosts would announce to the paying guests the list of rugby internationals who were present in their company. On several occasions there would be no mention of me or my female team mates. Again, telling us that we have no value. But that is starting to change and I now walk into events not with an embarrassed and hesitant shuffle but a confident, head-up stride. In 2017, I spent time in Hong Kong doing some corporate work around the Sevens (I managed to watch very little Sevens, which was a success for me obviously. I will never be able to get to grips with the game that has less than half the players but the same amount of space as the fifteens game. I am also not sure if Olympic inclusion has been overly positive, but more of that later in this book). One evening Jeremy and I attended a big Doddie Weir fundraising dinner. There were so many high-profile rugby players in attendance: Brian O'Driscoll, George Gregan, Jason Leonard, Gregor Townsend, Sean Fitzpatrick, the list goes on and on. At the end of the evening all of the rugby legends, as they were described, were called up to stand on stage and my name was included on that list. I was the only female rugby player there but I was treated with equality and parity and I thought, Yes, I should be on this stage. This is right.

This equality is still not common but at least we are seeing glimpses.

This drip-feed message, that we were not good enough, that we had no value, appeared everywhere and more often than not was amplified by our own rugby unions, the national governing bodies responsible for the overall development of the game – for everyone. In 2005 we toured New Zealand. The World Cup was a year away and this tour would form a crucial part of our preparation. To go and play the best in the world on their own territory would be tough. Boy, was it tough. We played the first of two tests at Eden Park before the men's National Provincial Championship (NPC) final between Auckland and Otago. We were playing a full international and the two teams on show that day were arguably the first and third placed teams in the world (France was probably second at the time, but this was in the days before official seedings for women's rugby – just another message that we were not as worthy). Theoretically this was one of *the* tests of 2005 in the world for women's rugby, but there was very minimal mention of our game in the match programme. There was a third of a page team-sheet; no introduction or explanation apart from the title 'Curtain Raiser' along with one sentence of welcome within a wider piece about the NPC game. There was no mention at all in the main introduction on the front page. The programme, A4 in size and thirty-eight pages, was surely long enough to offer at least some kind of explanation for our presence at Eden Park that day.

We did not fare much better back on home soil. Earlier that year we'd taken on Scotland at Twickenham in the Six Nations prior to the equivalent men's fixture. It was my first time playing at the revered ground in an England shirt. There was a lovely ninety-six-page programme for the occasion, with a grand total of three pages set aside for us, just over 3 per cent. On the front page of the programme Malcolm Phillips, the then president of the RFU, provided an introduction and welcome (or someone in the office wrote something that he put his name to). There was no mention of us. Zero. Of the three pages that were ours, one page was entirely devoted to an update on Scotland women. Good, but nothing about us? Seriously? There was also no mention of our game on the match ticket.

I remember an article written by a female sports journalist about her experience, a couple of years later, trying to get in to watch the women's game that was after the men's that day. The deal was that it was free to enter at the end of the men's match. Great, but perhaps it would have been a good idea to let the stadium stewards know this piece of information. The journalist spoke to several stewards who had no idea that a women's game was even taking place. It is also so frustrating subsequently hearing stories of supporters who had attended the men's game and who would have stayed on to watch the women's game if they'd known it was on. Blissfully unaware, they left the stadium along with the majority of others with no idea that the more successful of the English teams in action that day was about to take to the pitch.

For the first few years of my England career, the thing that meant so much, to wear the Red Rose with pride while representing England, did not come to fruition. Our red rose looked more like a tulip. We were not allowed to sport the official rose emblem. I am sure there were legal, copyright issues at stake and as the RFUW at the time was separate from the RFU it was clearly not deemed appropriate that we could share the emblem. The more feminine rose symbol that became so synonymous with English rugby was reserved exclusively for the boys at that time. The rose, the national flower of England, is a symbol of hope, prosperity and unity. United we were not, but it has certainly brought the RFU prosperity through official branding since 1998. We did eventually become wearers of the official rose in 2008. Now, the RFU widely promotes the women's team as the Red Roses and it's a good job we were elevated to sharing the rose – the Red Tulips does not have quite the same ring.

I am not bitter that I did not get paid to play for England; as I have already explained, I like the credibility that comes with telling the story of hard work, of working against the grain, of reaching heights without the support that others get. What I am bitter about is the lack of opportunity and the inequality that still exists for me post-retirement. Yes, I have been lucky enough to commentate on a number of games including two World Cup tournaments, but opportunities for female rugby media commentators or studio experts are still very few and far between. We are very rarely allowed to commentate on men's games, although of course men can commentate on women's games. I don't care whether commentators are male or female but I strongly believe that men and women should be able to commentate on both men's and women's rugby. We play by exactly the same laws, we play the same game, but for some reason because we are female we are given the message that we don't know enough to comment on men's rugby. There are glimmers of hope however; Emily Scarratt is starting to forge ahead and I am sure will be a regular on our screens, having also delivered some work on men's rugby. Maggie has also delivered commentary on some men's rugby Six Nations games and Nolli Waterman is a natural on TV, appearing on our TV screens and media outlets with more frequency as each day passes. For me, though, this won't happen. My face does not fit any more. And actually, for reasons that will become clearer, I will take this as a blessing in disguise. I don't need to continue to be immersed in this world. It is not good for me. If people want me to work they can ask me, but I am no longer going to seek out the doors. One day I may even shut my own door.

Chapter Seven
Mud, Maul, Mascara

'You play rugby? You're too pretty to play rugby.' I love it when I am told that; I really should not but I do. I am a girl and we girls love a compliment, whether we deem it to be true or not. It is nice to feel pretty, and it is even nicer to be given such a compliment. This should not be a compliment of course; it should annoy me. Why should it matter what I look like? I have directly and indirectly been trying to raise the profile of women's rugby for most of my life whilst striving to cement the view that, yes, you can be a girl and play rugby. Mud, mauls and mascara are not mutually exclusive, as some seem to think.

Whilst I, with some guilt, love the 'too pretty to play rugby' comment, at the other end of the scale I hate the, 'Ooh, I would not like to get on the wrong side of you' or, 'I wouldn't like to run in to you' or, 'You have really big hands' comments, especially when I am at a function trying to look attractive in an evening dress. This does not make me feel feminine or pretty; it just makes me feel down. Being big and scary on the rugby pitch is fine, but when I am out for an evening please believe me that it is not the look I am going for! I don't actually want to feel like a giant when I am in civvies. So whilst my size – 5'10½", 90kg-plus and a size sixteen (now in retirement creeping up to a size eighteen but doing my best to curtail that) – has helped me in my rugby career, I have struggled slightly with it when I am just being me. An ex of mine told me that I had really big arms when he was trying to chat me up in a bar. I should have known that it would not last and after seven years on and off we went our separate ways.

In 2004, when I had just broken into the main England team, I remember attending a very cold, wet and windy England training session on the top pitch at Newbury RFC. We were preparing for a two-game test series against Canada. The forwards coach, Graham Smith, brought the forwards together and had quite a stern and honest talk with us all. In this huddle, I was standing next to Rachel Vickers, who was one of our second rows, and in my opinion one of the most feminine and elegant members of the squad. Graham told us, in no uncertain terms, that if we were not prepared to have the big necks that we would develop through additional and specific strength training then we should not be there. Vickers and I just looked at each other and I have to be honest I thought, No way. I would do anything to play for England, but I don't think I was prepared to look like a man to get on the pitch.

I spent hours in the gym throughout my England career improving strength scores and building muscle, but I was still very much a woman. I built my strength naturally, with no supplements, enhancing my curvy, female body. It was important to me that I was still identified as a woman as well as a rugby player. Why? Because I like being a girl.

Simple. I am a girl and I am not going to apologise for that, not now or ever. Quite the opposite – I want to celebrate it. Graham learned a lot about women over the next ten years! He wanted us to be the best athletes we could be. He spent hours and days away from home travelling the country to deliver small-group skills sessions. I and my team mates benefitted massively from these sessions, but over time he also came to learn that for many of us our femininity was important too. Graham was a fantastic coach, a great person and deserves many more plaudits than he ever received. But there were many people who didn't understand that our femininity was important, and surprisingly many of these were women.

I speak to countless women who are sporty, who say that they want to try a different sport, or I meet women who are rugby supporters and enjoy the men's game so I suggest that maybe they have a go at rugby, and I get what has become a very standard response: they laugh in my face and say of course not, they are not built to play rugby. But what does this really mean? Rugby is one of the only sports that really does suit any body shape. There is a position on the pitch to suit anyone, no matter how tall, short, curvy or slim. So why am I constantly told by women that they are not built to play rugby? Because of this perception of rugby, that it is played by big, strong, strapping men, and consequently if you are female and you play you also have to be big or masculine. Our England captain in 2006 was an amazing player called Jo Yapp: a phenomenal player, a leader, and at just 5'3" with a petite frame to go with it she was one of the smallest on the pitch – and, in fact, is smaller than most of the female population generally. This is one of the best things about rugby; really anyone can play. I am sure that the same goes for men, and that there are many men out there who do not play because they think that they are not big enough. Actually, if you stand next to our current men's international players you will be surprised at how many of them are not that big. But the way the game is marketed and perceived works against one of the most valuable attractions of our great game: that there is a place for anyone, whoever you are, wherever you are from, whatever you look like and however big or small, tall or short you are. Sadly, I believe that the beautiful essence of the game is being gradually destroyed by the perceived need for bigger muscles and the gym culture.

I have been insulted so many times by different people I have spoken to over the years, young and old. Not intentionally I suspect, but unthinking all the same. On one occasion at a rugby event I was speaking to a man whose daughter used to play rugby but at age fourteen she had stopped. When I asked him why, he explained that she liked boys and make-up, so she couldn't play rugby. Why on earth not? I like boys, I like make-up – are you telling me that I need to stop playing rugby? He didn't intend to hurt my feelings but I wanted to shout and scream whenever people said things like this to me. I was personally hurt, but I was also hurt for the game.

And then we move on to the elephant in the room, the taboo subject. That, as I play rugby, I must be a lesbian. I have been asked directly by men if I am a lesbian when I have told them that I play rugby. One of the best things about rugby is its inclusivity and I would never want that to change. What I would also not want to change is that the world of women's rugby is clearly an environment in which people can feel comfortable and safe being who they are. But what I do want to be clear about is that women's rugby does not just attract one kind of woman. There are many of us out there. Some of us who like men, some who like women and some who like both! But what is important is that it does not matter. What matters is the sport, and the sport's ability to allow and encourage participants the freedom to be themselves. I go into this in more detail later in the book when I talk about the power of rugby. But please do not judge us by what you think it means to be female and to play rugby.

Even now at the age of forty I am still very sensitive about comments about being girly. I don't spend hours putting make-up on every morning, but I will put mascara on when I am going out – hence the title of this book. I don't spend every day in heels, but I love an excuse to wear them for an evening out or to a work event. I own countless pairs of trousers and jeans and I often chuck on a pair of trackies, but I also wear dresses and skirts and when I do I really enjoy it. I love my bags and scarves and heels, and I love being a woman. I have also played rugby for most of my life. And that is completely fine!

Typing this book now is actually a little challenging due to the long nails I have grown, having finally, properly, hung my boots up. I proudly showed them off to my sister-in-law recently like a young kid showing off a new toy! It was also only relatively recently that I got my ears pierced. At the ripe old age of thirty-seven I sat in a Claire's Accessories shop window in a seat normally occupied by girls at least thirty years younger and paid to have two holes put in my ears. I had wanted to get my ears pierced when I was about thirteen but my mum refused and said that if I still wanted to get them done when I was sixteen then I could. By the time I was fourteen I was playing rugby regularly, and as the two do not mix well I never got around to getting it done. Now I love them. Just putting on a pair of earrings makes me feel so elegant and feminine.

I say again, I would have always played rugby; I just happen to have been born female. If my twin brother was born female I am sure that he would still have played rugby. This apparent distinction between being a girl and playing rugby is something that I have struggled with, and I have also struggled with why it matters what other people think of me. Why am I so sensitive to the thought that strangers don't think I am feminine, based on the one fact that I played rugby? And what is more important to me – being identified as a woman or being identified as a rugby player? The answer? Both.

I set up my own company called Inspiring Women. Inspiring Women is a speaker agency 'Putting Female Voices First' – a platform to find and encourage more female speakers. I am passionate about encouraging female leaders through the use of sport, and one of the charity projects I am involved with through Tag Rugby Trust, 'Female Inspiration Through Rugby', does just that. I strongly believe that anyone, regardless of gender, should have the opportunity to choose – whether that is to play a sport, to take up a hobby, to pursue a certain career – but I also accept that men and women are different. We are physiologically different in some fairly obvious ways (I have spent a fortune on sports bras over the years) but I think that we are generally a little different emotionally too. And guess what? That is OK. In fact, it is more than OK. But we can still play rugby, despite people telling us consciously or subconsciously that we can't.

On one occasion I was part of a radio debate for 5 Live. I was in the studio with Nicky Ponsford (the RFU's head of women's performance) in Bath, linked up to Tony Livesy in the main studio in London and a man who will remain nameless (because luckily for him I can't remember who it was) who was linking in from Manchester. Radio 5 had successfully managed to bring on board one of the most ignorant, chauvinistic people I have had the pleasure to chat to. It was a good job that we were many miles apart because after he told me that women should be in the kitchen whilst their husbands played or watched sport I may not have been accountable for my actions if he was in the same studio space. When I offered him *free* tickets to one of our Six Nations games live on air he declined. He said that women could not play rugby. When I asked him if he had ever watched a game of women's rugby he confirmed that he had not. Such ignorance. I am not a fan of football, in fact I really can't see the appeal, but that does not mean that I think that people should not be able to play football.

And some discrimination was subtler than that. Forever being told to play on the bottom pitch, or only use the tiniest corner of the training pitch, or to play on a Sunday afternoon when no one is around the club, or to be allowed to play at Twickenham maybe once a year but not have your game promoted or marketed. To constantly read about England's record-breaking victory or to read tweets about an international Eight scoring a 'record-breaking' number of tries – make that 'male international' – when they haven't scored as many as the women's team or me personally. No record broken there then. To hear our game referred to as 'women's rugby' – fine, but be even-handed and refer to the rugby played by men as 'men's rugby'. To be invited to rugby events and dinners and then be sat at the back while having to listen to the boys talk. This all adds up, this all tells us that we are not good enough because we happen to be female. These seemingly small things are really impactful when experienced over and over again.

Recently, however, I scored a victory and reduced the number of these little occurrences by one. I was getting extremely frustrated at seeing announcements for the upcoming RPA awards. They were announcing England Woman Player of the Year and so on alongside England Player of the Year. This is wrong. If we put the gender against the awards for women, then the same should be happening for men's awards. After a series of communications with both the RFU and the RPA the awards were referred to as England Women and England Men. Yes, thank you, a little victory. I will of course be checking yearly that this remains the case.

Writing this I ask myself that if I had a pre-birth supernatural power would I have ensured I was born male so that I would not have faced all of this discrimination over the years? So that I could have been famous and in possession of a significantly larger bank balance? The answer is no. Not because I don't want to be male but because I do like being a woman. I liked being a girl when I was growing up and I like being a woman now. I also tell people that I enjoyed playing rugby at the particular time that I did. To experience the growth and development of the game first hand and know that you have had a direct impact on that is heart-warming. Yes, it could also be frustrating but looking at the bigger picture I am happy about the time that I played. I have enjoyed converting men's rugby supporters, to purely rugby supporters; and in my recent years I have enjoyed promoting female leadership and sporting success stories through my company Inspiring Women. And if I had not been born female I would not have experienced the highs and lows of my formerly disastrous but more recently very happy love life! My search for Mr Right, like my rugby journey, was also rather like a roller coaster. There were many troughs. It did take a few years for me to successfully navigate myself down an aisle and I do wonder how harshly my rugby career impacted on my quest to find love and happiness.

Chapter Eight
The Elusive Mr Right

Throughout school and university, I would often talk with friends about what our lives would be like when we were thirty, an age that seemed so far away but at the same time quite appealing. For me I knew that I would be living in a nice house by the sea, I would have two or three children and a husband, a nice garden with weekend breaks away, Sunday afternoon family walks, the gorgeous aroma of freshly baked bread in the kitchen and a vase of fresh flowers on the table! When I reached the age of thirty none of this had happened. It was 25 May 2009 when the fateful day came around and I was dreading it. I was dreading it because in my mind my life was not set up, I had no husband or children and I didn't have an established career. I was, however, at the prime of my rugby career, a successful captain and just over a year out from the next World Cup. On the pitch things were going well, but I was still that girl who dreamed of growing a family, of walking hand in hand with the person I love on a Sunday afternoon in the beautiful English countryside, of living in a lovely home with lovely wallpaper, of going on romantic weekend breaks, of having nice clothes, of being slimmer, of being fitter. When my thirtieth birthday came around I did have a fairly long-term boyfriend but it was not the steadiest of relationships and I believe we were on some kind of break at the time. For the purposes of this book we are calling him 'Mr Nearly Right'.

Mr Nearly Right and I met in 2005 in New Zealand on a tram in Wellington whilst we were both out supporting the British and Irish Lions. He was just my type, a big rugby guy and, to me, really good-looking. After our eyes met on the tram, we kept randomly bumping into each other over the next couple of days. It really felt like it was meant to be. He was the ex who had said to me, 'Wow, you have really big arms'; not the best chat-up line. Obviously what he should have said was something along the lines of, 'Your arms are so toned, you are the most beautiful, elegant and athletic woman I have ever seen.' But I knew he was trying to be complimentary so I let him off. We saw each other a lot during the tour and then continued to see each other a lot when we got home. We went out for a couple of years then broke up. He didn't want the commitment of a long-term relationship – we were living a couple of hours apart, he in Surrey and me in Bristol, and we went our separate ways but we stayed in contact. I went out with another guy for a couple of years (Mr Too Nice) but I missed my ex and I knew I wanted to get back together; so, I found out, did he.

We got back together in 2009 and stayed together for another three years. I thought we would get married, get a house together, start a family. At the time, to me he was my Mr Right, but unfortunately not right enough and I was not his Mrs Right. When we broke up for the second time I still thought I loved him, but I was not in love with him, and until this happened to us I never thought that really existed – the difference between loving someone and being 'in' love. I thought it was just something that Oprah or Trisha (some of you will be too young to know who Trisha is. Don't worry, just let us oldies relish our memories!) talked about, but it does exist. It is a real thing. Perhaps I didn't work at our love enough. Was that why we were not *in* love? Could we have been in love forever and grown old together like we so often used to speak about?

When I look back now I see that our whole relationship was really based around when I could see him, when I could fit him into my schedule, followed by immense disappointment when he couldn't or didn't want to see me when I was free. I used to read this as him letting me down, but looking back, everything was based around me. This must have been hard for him to manage. I know that he was really proud of my rugby achievements; he supported me in his own way and I do know that he loved me. But I was the boss throughout our whole relationship. I didn't necessarily want to be but that was how it worked out. It had to be because of course I was following that selfish dream of mine . . . to win a World Cup.

Before Mr Nearly Right there was Mr Not Right At All. Now, he is an interesting one! He was my first real boyfriend after seeing a few guys casually at university. He was shorter than me, had completely opposite political views and was a royalist – I am not; he once stood me up because of the Queen. He didn't go on a date with her, obviously, but he had a date with the TV and a programme about the Queen. We came from pretty different backgrounds, but we did have rugby in common and at the time that was enough. Rugby draws people together from so many different backgrounds; that is one of the best things about it. He asked me out a few times and I said no. I could not really deal with the height thing (he was a lot shorter than me) and then one day I said yes. I don't really know why, which I guess is not the greatest basis for a relationship, but we were together for nearly three years, albeit with an eleven-month break in the middle while I went off travelling. I kind of dealt with the height thing; I wore flats a lot! Mr Not Right At All and I were never meant to grow old together but I guess I did learn a few relationship lessons and I learned how to deal with a bit of heartache when we broke up.

Mr Cool was the first boy I kissed. Aged ten in the dare corner at junior school. He was the first boy I sent a love letter to (yes, a letter, written on paper with a pen – no such thing as text messaging or social media back then) and then denied all knowledge of it when his twin brother asked on his behalf whether it was me who had sent it. Seriously, Catherine, if you deny writing it then what was the point? Anyway, we did eventually become official – which meant that we walked to swimming together every Friday and occasionally held hands. He was pretty damn cool too and earned me big street-cred points – I was not overly cool aged ten, and still am not some thirty years later – but I was rubbish at developing our relationship. When he asked if I could go round to his house for a party which my brother Gregory was going to, I said no. I said no to a guy I really liked! Why? This was something I did a few times subsequently – most significantly to Mr Why On Earth Did I Say No, who really should be named Mr Right. We will come on to him later.

Every girl has to experience one Holiday Romance during their life; it is kind of a road junction that needs to be crossed before continuing on your way. My junction occurred when I was on a Club 18–30s holiday in Magaluf – classy. It was in the summer of 1998 and a few university friends and I packed ourselves off to Majorca. My parents were a bit unsure as to what a Club 18–30s holiday was, but seemed to be OK with it. The hotel that we stayed in certainly cemented the expression 'you get what you pay for' – but ever the optimist I said how good it was that we were staying in that particular hotel because when we were in it we didn't have to look at it. At least it did have a pool, which came in handy as the water to our rooms was regularly switched off. The guy who used to sit in the corner of reception every day pleasuring himself just added to the overall effect. After a week I thought it would be good to write a postcard home. The only thing I felt worthy of mention to my parents – 'Dear Parents, Hot here, tomorrow we might be going on a boat ride, hope you are well, love from Catherine.' That boat ride was a trip out on a banana boat; two of my friends banged heads and got concussion and I strained my arm muscles from fear of falling off – which is clearly the whole point. I have never been a fan of water.

After about five days of experiencing 'Spanish' culture we were in a bar when I heard the sexy tones of a young man from Wolverhampton who subsequently became Mr Holiday Romance. As the holiday drew to a close I had enough sense to understand that I needed to draw this particular life experience to a close. So on the romantic setting of a sunlounger on the beach at night-time under the light of the moon with only a couple of people in the near distance throwing up due to too much sangria, I explained to Mr Holiday Romance that we would not be seeing each other on our return to the UK. Our love was only right for the environs of Magaluf, and although he was lovely I did not want to ruin what we had by taking it back to Blighty. By keeping it as a cherished memory we would have it forever. Or something like that. Mr Holiday Romance was fairly persistent though, sending me cards, mix tapes (oh, for the days of mix tapes), letters and then phoning me up one day telling me he was going to move to Cardiff where I was at university. Things were getting worrying. I was becoming fearful that my holiday romance that every girl should go through was becoming something real that I was going to have to deal with . . . Until – hooray! – luckily Mr Holiday Romance got sent to prison and I didn't have to worry. Something about selling dodgy T-shirts but quite frankly I didn't ask in case it was something more serious. For the next few years I was largely single but, without going into detail, because my parents will be reading this, I can say that I enjoyed life. But really, rugby was becoming the main love interest in my life and, like building any relationship, it was starting to take up more and more of my time.

Because Mr Nearly Right and I were together for several years and because of my rugby commitments, my experience of one of life's rich experiences – the world of Internet dating – didn't come until I was into my thirties. Along the way I met Mr I Want To Be A Student Layabout Forever; Mr Cat Man (as in he pawed me like a cat in the cinema, not that he owned cats); Mr One-Armed With Emotional And Psychological Challenges; Mr Twenty Years Older Than He Said; Mr Arrogant And Alcoholic And Selfish But I Thought I Could Save Him; Mr Practice Man (come on, everyone needs to practise before embarking on the real thing); Mr Talk About His Daughter And Nothing Else; Mr Move To India (really he could have just said that he didn't want to see me again). And this list is not even mentioning a whole raft of men who did not even make it to an actual date. Internet dating was awful, but without it I would not have met my Mr Right in 2014. Mr Right, who for two years was named Mr Why On Earth Did I Say No.

Before Mr Why On Earth Did I Say No and I met in person we spoke on the phone, for hours and hours each night. I loved those phone calls and I was amazed at how close I could feel to someone without having met them face to face. I was equally surprised at how excited I used to get before our phone calls. I knew that something special was happening. We went for our first date in High Wycombe. Why on earth would two relatively sane people go on a date in High Wycombe, I hear you ask, but I was staying there to deliver a talk at a function at Adams Park – you know, that place situated geographically closer to London than Coventry, where the team formerly known as London Wasps played their rugby. Mr Why On Earth Did I Say No picked me up from my hotel in his freshly valeted car (how romantic) and drove me to the centre of High Wycombe. I liked the look of him as soon as I saw him. He was nearly as big as his car (impressive as his car was a Nissan Qashqai), but as a powerlifter this was to be expected. Walking to the restaurant beside him I felt petite. Me, Catherine Spencer, felt petite. This had never happened before. Even when I was born I was heavier than my twin brother. One massive tick for my date. We had a couple of drinks (not too many) and something to eat and conversation flowed really well. I liked him! What was happening? Dates were so much easier when it was obvious that the guy was not normal. Far fewer decisions to make; just a nice simple, 'No, I do not want to see you again.'

But not this time. It was decided that we would go on a second date. Well, actually our first date. High Wycombe was just a pre-first date because Mr Why On Earth Did I Say No wanted to check me out before allowing me to go on an official first date with him. It was a good date – he booked a massage for me which was bliss, while he waited patiently for me. I didn't get free massages any more after retiring, and my rugby-ravaged body still craved them but my wallet said no. I was starting to think, There must be something wrong with this guy because he is being so nice to me. After the massage we went to the Lobster Shack restaurant (posh for me!) and then bowling. It was by all accounts a pretty good date. So why on earth did I tell him I did not want to go on a third date with him? I was carrying on the trend I started aged ten when I told Mr Cool that I didn't want to go to his party. If I'd known in 2014 what I do now, there is no way on this earth that I would have said no to a third date. I could try and psychoanalyse myself to work out why I made that decision or I can just be forever thankful that Mr Why On Earth Did I Say No reconnected with me and ultimately became my Mr Right and now my official Mr The Man that my eyes locked with as I walked down the aisle on 29 December 2017.

For most of my adult 'relationship' life until Mr Right I had been the one in charge, I had made all of the decisions, but, aged thirty-eight, I realised that I craved a man who would sometimes take charge instead, who would look after me for a change. I had more or less had enough of being in charge in every aspect of my life. Yes, I am a leader, and yes, I enjoy that – but not all the time. Behind closed doors, in my mind, I just want to be looked after. I am vulnerable, I am a girl who is afraid of the dark, who is afraid of spiders, a girl who sometimes wants to feel like a princess, who wants to feel girly and feminine. More importantly I don't want to feel guilty for wanting to feel girly and feminine.

I did become that princess for the day. I did walk down that aisle. I do go for walks hand in hand with the man I love, we have a new house – not in the country yet but that will happen one day. Lovely wallpaper will also be pasted at some point! And the family bit? Well, that has not happened just yet and it is quite possible that it never will. This year I will be forty, and with no children yet I wonder if I made the biggest sacrifice of all. Was my rugby career worth it? I dream of my husband (I love saying the H-word) chopping wood in the garden of our country house whilst he is watching over our kids running around in wellies enjoying themselves and laughing. And there I am, looking out of the kitchen window, taking a break from baking amazing bread and seeing huge love on my husband's face for the family that is around him.

Those who know us personally will know how incredibly important that is to us. But at the time of writing no mini Spence has entered this world, and if one ever does, if we do manage to create a bump together, I will officially be a geriatric mum. Am I too old? I am still clinging on to the hope that we will have children, that I can give my Mr Right his family. I will be devastated if it does not happen. Though if it doesn't we will be getting that convertible that we want. We went and sat in one recently at a Mercedes dealership, pretending to be considering buying one. If we don't have kids we will definitely be embracing DINK life – Double Income No Kids!

I guess to some extent, apart from my family who I love unconditionally, there have been two main loves of my life: Man and Rugby. But how do we really know who or what we love, and what if they don't love us back? I got my lightning moment with Mr Right. I fell in love with him, I realise now, before we had even met, when we spent hours and hours talking on the phone. I then fell in love with him again when I experienced that thunderbolt, that amazing moment I thought only happened in the movies, in that instant when I opened my front door to him when we first met up again two years after our first couple of dates. When I opened the door that day I knew without certainty that we would be together forever. And I know that Mr Right loves me. I just know, and it is an amazing feeling. What I don't know with certainty is whether I really do love rugby any more and more significantly whether rugby loves me back. Sometimes I wonder about the way that rugby has treated me. Surely rugby can't love me.

I read a book recently that introduced me to the theory

of love created by a psychologist called Zick Rubin. He determined that love is formed of three components. The first is attachment, which describes our emotional need for the other person. I have this in bucketloads with Mr Right. The second is caring – Rubin describes this as our need to give to the other person. Again, I have bucketloads of care for Mr Right. The third component is intimacy. Rubin states this as the need for close and confidential communication with another; Mr Right and I have shared so much with each other that we have not shared with anyone else in the same way.

Do I experience any of this with rugby? Rugby, the constant companion in my life through all of my relationship woes and Internet-dating disasters. Do I have an emotional need for rugby? Is there an attachment? I find myself drawn back to rugby again and again. Sometimes I want to escape, but I never quite do. I definitely care. I have given so much to the sport for selfish reasons but also for selfless causes. And is there a level of intimacy? I think so; rugby has been the cause of so much emotion, but you will know by now that this has not always been happy, positive or beneficial. It has not always felt like love. If I think really hard about this I understand now that I am not in love with rugby any more; I was but I am no longer. Just as my relationship ended with Mr Nearly Right, so too has my relationship with rugby ended, at that level anyway. This is a good thing. Accepting this has allowed me to let go and to see rugby in a new light. It has drained my emotion, it has drained resource, it has drained time. Rugby does not love me back.

I like rugby a lot, there is so much that is great about

it, but I no longer unconditionally love rugby. I am not *in* love with rugby. Admitting that to myself, writing this in print, has been a weight lifted from my shoulders. But it has taken the love of a person to help me see through the fog. I don't need to punish myself; I don't need to fight for there to be something more with rugby. I can simply like it for what it is now: a good sport that I happen to know quite a lot about. But I no longer need to give myself up to it.

And as thoughts of previous relationships start to dwindle once they are over, so too will my ties to rugby. As new chapters commence in my life, as I become happy to just be me, the pull to rugby becomes weaker. I do not crave the appearance of rugby in my life, I do not need its attention and nor, I am increasingly finding, do I want it. Whether I will break completely from all things rugby I don't know, but what I do know is that the thought is becoming increasingly appealing to me with every day that goes past. I do still crave the good old days of 2003, feeling excited watching the men win the World Cup, or the fun of 2001 and 2005, when I loved being part of the travelling Lions fans because I was 100 per cent a rugby fan. But the sport has changed and so have I. I can enjoy the memories but I know now that I will never again feel about rugby the way I did back then. It has been such a big part of my life that I feel guilty for not wanting it to continue to be. I still have the occasional thought of Mr Nearly Right. I hope he is happy. But I have no pull to him. I don't want him in my life. I don't feel guilty for having no feelings for him. One day this is how I need to feel about rugby – and I am getting there. My resource that I hand over to rugby, be it time or emotion, is now more controlled. Rugby no longer controls me. There are still moments when this is not quite the case, but generally I am now in control. I am for the most part where I want to be in this relationship: nearing the end and ready to say goodbye.

This was one of many squad pictures taken with my beloved Folkestone Ladies over the years. I am still in touch with most former teammates, and five of the players in this picture came to my wedding in 2017. Our two coaches, 'Daddy Caddy' on the right and 'Woody', fourth from left, were fantastic. They devoted so much time, energy and emotion to our team. Angela, stood next to me on the far left, was instrumental in setting up the team in the mid-nineties. I wonder how my life may have played out if it was not for Angela!

Photo: Ken Matcham

A few years ago Folkestone put together a calendar featuring different sections and members of the club. I joined some of the new Folkestone ladies players to show that we like to dress up and don our mascara as well as playing rugby.

Every year Folkestone played a 'marrieds' v 'singles' rugby match on boxing day – a good day to work out what was going on in people's love lives! It was always a match for the men but one year (after I had retired from England) I took the opportunity to play alongside my brothers, and it was a really special moment; the three of us on the pitch together. I played for about ten minutes but then subbed myself off when I was getting a little too involved in the rucks and mauls!

This was the first rugby game I played after retiring from England in 2011, playing for Aylesford in a local tournament at Ashford. The player supporting me in this photo is Maxine, one of my best friends. One of the reasons I chose to play back in Kent after retiring was to play alongside my closest friends again. Maxine played 7 and I played 8 for Folkestone for many years before playing together again at Aylesford.

This was the first play-off game that Aylesford were involved with against Thurrock. We beat them to move up into the premiership and Thurrock were demoted. Two years later the tables were turned and we were the premiership team playing for survival, but we beat them again (coming back from 17-nil down at half-time) to retain our premiership spot. Our third and final play-off game, before the Harlequins merger, was against Waterloo. I found some extra pace from somewhere to chase down the wing and tackle a Waterloo player who was on for a near match-winning try. I wonder if Harlequins would exist as they do now if I had not made that significant tackle to keep us in the premiership?

I think this was one of the muddiest rugby games I have ever played in; playing for Bristol against Darlington. Looking back now I don't think we should have played; there was so much water on the pitch it could have been dangerous, but we all came through fine. Many people pay for a mud pack and exfoliation in health spas across the country. My suggestion? Play rugby and you get it for free!

Photo: Gary Browne

This was me, very fresh-faced, working the local media in 2004. This was just a few days after I won my first cap for England. I possibly should have recruited a hair stylist!

With my parents after another Grand Slam victory. This was after our nail-biting match against France in 2010. I was very lucky to have such a supportive family. There were not many England games that I played without at least one member of my family in the crowd who I could give the 'nod' to before kick-off.

I 'ran' two marathons for Tag Rugby Trust, and on this second occasion Gregory also joined in. We ran the first half together until my knee gave way. I staggered the rest and Gregory ran his second half faster than the first. Typical! The man in the middle of this group is Martin Hansford, the chairman of TRT who, after finishing the marathon about two hours quicker than me, proceeded to run up Sacré-Cœur monument with his brother. I declined that particular après-marathon activity!

This photo was taken after our 2009 victory over the Black Ferns at Twickenham and my 50th cap. It was a good day and extra special to have Martin, Gregory and my parents there. This is one of very few rugby photos that I have printed and on display in our house.

I have been fortunate to have travelled to a number of countries with Tag Rugby Trust. In 2011 we headed to India where I took the opportunity to deliver some coaching in Calcutta. At this point I was sharing my extensive knowledge of backs moves and lines of running – it was not a long session!

Photo: Aimee Lister

Here I am assuming my normal anthem time stance, head down and eyes shut before a test against Uganda. 15-a-side matches are not common for Ugandan teams, so it was great to be able to put an invitation side together. Standing next to me is Lindsay Anfield, former Rugby League GB captain. We had been donated some Moody Cow shirts to wear for the match – the Moody Cows are an invitation team that have been running for several years. It was hot, the ground was not entirely level, but this remains one of my favourite ever games to have played in.

Photo: Aimee Lister

Claire Purdy, a former England team mate, also travelled out to Uganda to volunteer on the trip and play in the test. She even managed to get one of her signature spins in. She was a skilful prop and played an instrumental part in the try against the Black Ferns in 2009 at Twickenham making a great break down the wing.

Photo: Ellie Kealey, Sheeko Productions

When we headed to Ghana we were coaching coaches and teachers but we would often still find ourselves in the middle of large groups of curious kids. This can make the task of checking kit and counting up tag belts a little challenging!

Photo: Tag Rugby Trust

As part of our Female Inspiration Through Rugby project we have teamed up with an organisation called The Girls Legacy in Zimbabwe. The Girls Legacy have helped to train our FITR volunteers as facilitators and mentors. Here I am delivering a short talk at one of their conferences in Harare; at this conference we also introduced Tag Rugby to the delegates. Hundreds of young women and girls playing rugby delivered by our volunteers was a great sight.

Like all good number 8s – clearly using the scrum as an opportunity to save some energy!

Don't leave microphones lying around, otherwise I am likely to pick them up! This was the end of a schools and community club tournament in Uganda.

I love this photo, which was taken as part of a local Shepway Sports Trust project. The photographer, Lucy, took a number of photos of various sports men and women across the area. We took this photo on a very, very, very windy day at Dungeness – a pretty exposed part of the South East coast. After this I asked Lucy if she happened to do wedding photos… luckily she said 'yes!'

I am very proud of my Inspiring Women logo. The idea of looking up is such a key message of mine that I wanted it integrated into the logo. Having an ex who was a graphic designer proved pretty useful!

Photo: Lucy Mohr

I didn't want our wedding to be overrun with rugby guests, but I was really pleased that Graham Smith, Sophie Hemming, Julia Hutton and Maggie Alphonsi were able to attend. Claire Purdy also arrived a little later.

Photo: Lucy Mohr

I loved every second of our wedding day; from the moment I woke up, to getting ready, to walking down the aisle, to taking photos on the canal bank, to our reception and even the embarrassing speeches. I really would not change a thing.

Photo: Lucy M

I love getting my make-up done whether it is befor media appearance or, as shown here, on the morn of my wedding day. I definitely felt like a princess this day!

Photo: Getty Images

ing against Wales in 2007 during our Tulip Rose days. This was before we were allowed to share the England Rose the men use. This was also in the good old days of baggier playing shirts! We went on to win the Grand Slam this , the second of five slams for me and six Championship titles.

Me and Maggie at the end of the 2010 World Cup final. I can't tell you how many times these few moments have been replayed in my head as a different version, one in which we were waiting to lift the trophy. Maggie of course did go on to do just that in 2014.

I was always used as a lifter rather than jumper in the lineout, and I think this shows why! Heather Fisher and Claire Purdy managing to get me off the ground a little bit with the 2011 trophy after my last game. George Rozario looking on doing nothing to help – typical back!

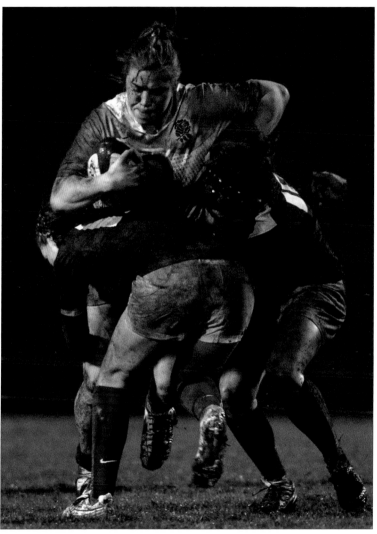

Photo: Getty Images

Another classic 6 Nations France test. This image is taken from our 2010 fixture played in France. There was a great atmosphere, as there always was in France, and the weather was perfect. By that I mean it was raining and muddy! We won this game by just a single point 11–10. France had a shot at goal in the last play but fortunately for us they missed, resulting in us going on to win yet another Grand Slam – scoring 156 points for, and just 15 against, across the tournament that season.

Photo: PA Images

This photo was taken just seconds after the whistle blew at the end of our Ireland 6 Nations match in 2011 and the curtain was drawn on my England career. Little did I know then how tough retirement was going to be but, judging by this image, I was starting to get a taste.

Chapter Nine

The Captaincy

It was a conversation with the outgoing captain, Sue Day (Daisy), that really started my England captaincy journey. After the 2006 World Cup there were several retirees, including the captain Jo Yapp and our superstar winger Kim Shaylor; both were too young to need to retire, but were making life choices that were not compatible with international rugby. Sue Day was one of the players who carried on playing until the 2007 Six Nations and she took over the captaincy. I knew that Daisy was retiring from fifteen-a-side rugby at the end of the 2007 tournament, which would leave a big leadership gap. I had quietly been developing my confidence as a player and had become the first choice at number 8. I had very slowly also been developing as a leader of sorts. I captained my home club Folkestone before leaving after the 2006 World Cup and had also become a player rep for England. Looking back, it was a very ineffective role due to little support or communication or interest from the powers-that-be, but it felt important at the time and a step up for me. I had captained my university side and also the Welsh Universities team. But I only started to think about the England captaincy when I knew Daisy was retiring. Until I spoke to her I had not mentioned my building desire to be captain to anyone. Not my family, not even my twin brother.

Only twice before had the suggestion of England captaincy been mentioned; the first time I laughed it away; the second time I had no idea about until a recent conversation with my dad. The first time was during a slightly alcohol-fuelled conversation with one of my university team mates Speedy Sarah (she was a winger) in a bar in Manly, Sydney, in 2001. The Lions squad were in there and the two of us, along with my brother and another of our friends, found ourselves in the same place, a complete chance encounter as we had no idea that they would be there. I think it was Dai Young that we were talking to at the time when Speedy Sarah confidently announced that I would one day be England captain. I told her not to be silly. I may have had a couple of beers but I was still thinking straight. This was in 2001 before I even thought about attempting to play for England. I am sure Dai Young does not remember this, neither I am sure do Brian O'Driscoll, Matt Dawson or Dan Luger. Ronan O'Gara may possibly recall being annoyed at yet another rugby fan asking about those punches that he received in that infamous tour game against New South Wales Waratahs, but Jonny Wilkinson probably does not remember Gregory and I excitedly telling him that we shared his birthday; Jeremy Guscott undoubtedly does not recall the dismissive look that he gave me as I was invading their space. Scott Gibbs and Rob Henderson probably do both remember their singing that night; I know that Rob does as I have since spoken to him about it. It was a proper rugby night out! And now I find myself sharing the stage with some of these same people or their former team mates. How the world changes and twists and turns.

The second occasion was in 2003. The England coach Geoff Richards had phoned me on the landline at my parents' house (this was pre-mobile phone for me). Apparently he phoned several times until he finally got through to me when I was in. I can't remember what this call was about but I assume it was to do with Elite Squad selection. On one of his first attempts he spoke to my dad. My parents were great – they never pushed me and never pushed coaches into making decisions – but my dad did say to Geoff that he thought that one day I would make a good England captain. I never knew that this conversation had taken place until 2018 when we were reminiscing following my Honorary Doctorate ceremony in Canterbury. Geoff had retired by the time I was awarded the captaincy by Gary Street, but Geoff had a huge influence on my career. Importantly he liked my style of rugby, he helped me realise what my strengths were and allowed me the time to develop as a player and a person in the England shirt. I owe a lot to Geoff, as does the women's game.

Back to 2007 – I phoned Daisy and I guess I was after some reassurance that I was not going mad, that I was not deluding myself in thinking that I could take the armband. When I suggested to Daisy that I call the newly appointed head coach Gary Street and tell him that I would like to be considered, she said absolutely, yes, I should. That would be a move that would single me out as a leader – that I could be brave and put my hand up. This notion of putting your hand up has stayed with me and is now a core focus for Inspiring Women.

During a lunchbreak from work I plucked up the courage. I drove to a car park in Chipping Sodbury, which was not far from where I worked, to make the call to Streety. Sitting in a Nissan Micra in a car park did not feel like the right setting but I had time between meetings and if I didn't do it then, I am not sure if I ever would have done. I was really, really nervous but made myself hit the call button. What followed was a general conversation about the England captaincy and a discussion about three other players who I thought could potentially do the job – Rochelle Clark, Maggie Alphonsi and Tamara Taylor. Tamara was my first choice; although Rocky and Maggie were and are leaders, it was Tam, in my opinion, who had the ability to lead in different situations both on and off the pitch without it affecting her own game. I do remember mentioning myself but not with the air of confidence I was hoping for. Yet by making that call I got myself on the shortlist and that was the key.

Seven months later I was in the living room of the house I shared in Bristol, getting ready to drive up to club training with Worcester, when Streety phoned me. We had no summer tour that year and the next game following the last match of the Six Nations in March was a friendly against the USA in December so the new captain to replace Sue Day had yet to be announced. Streety's first words were something like, 'Hi, Spence, what are you up to over the next few months?' I thought this was a pretty strange thing to ask; he knew exactly what I was up to and it mostly revolved around sleeping, eating, training, playing and working. He then said, 'Well, your life is about to get a whole load busier, because you are the new England captain.' I could not believe it!

When I put the phone down I texted Streety straight back just to check that I had not dreamed the conversation. There was a big mirror above the mantelpiece and I remember just gazing into it thinking, Wow – I am looking at the England captain and it is me in the mirror! It is such a vivid memory, staring at myself and taking in, for a few minutes, just what this could mean. And then I remembered I had to get a move on and drive to training! It seemed that I had ticked more boxes than any of the others I had mentioned in that previous call, so I got the nod. If I had not made that call I don't know if I would have even been on the shortlist. Sometimes all it takes is a little bit of short-term bravery just to put your hand up that will change your whole future.

The next two weeks were even stranger for me because the RFUW wanted to issue a press release on the new captaincy but wanted to wait until closer to our upcoming December USA game so we were not competing with men's autumn international media. This meant that I could not tell anyone apart from my close family. This was really tough but at the same time quite nice. I felt proud of myself that I was the new captain; I could enjoy the personal pride before the hard work started – and boy, was it hard.

Inside I was a shaking, nervous wreck. Outside I was a strong confident leader, of sorts. I didn't really know what a good leader was though. I thought Martin Johnson was pretty good because of his aura on the pitch. Where he went, people followed. He was always there on the front line. I am not sure that he was the most eloquent of captains and actually if he had been female and playing women's rugby then he would not have been selected, because he did not have the right media presence. However, I wanted that aura. I often say that a good leader will turn around and see her team following; a great leader doesn't need to turn around to know that they are following; but an excellent leader will be happy if other players are ahead. Empowering and strengthening others is such a key leadership skill. One of the key leadership lessons that I learned was that I didn't have to do everything all of the time and I didn't have to please everyone all of the time. It took a huge weight of built-up internal expectation and pressure off my shoulders. This release allowed me to be 100 per cent me rather than trying to be something or someone else. A lot is said about authentic leadership and this was when I understood what that meant.

One of the first decisions I made as captain was to turn down the offer of Sue Day as mentor. She is a good, intelligent person whom I respect greatly, but I did not want to be like her. I think that mentoring is a really powerful tool but I needed to be my own captain, my own leader. I gradually came to understand who I was as a leader, but for the first couple of years I was winging it. I rarely received feedback as a captain in the way that I did as a player, so it was difficult to understand if I was doing a good job. I had to recognise my own signs. I had to learn to analyse my own performance as captain. This was a challenge for two reasons: firstly, I was still learning what good leadership was, and secondly, this was set against a backdrop of my own limited self-belief as a leader made worse by the opinions of some other players who did not feel that Streety had made the right decision. Eighteen months into my captaincy, during the 2009 Six Nations, my decision-making and assertion as captain came into question; another three months on and my captaincy was starting to become very fragile, weakened by my own emotions and chipped away at by others. It was tough.

My first game as captain was to begin at 2:30 p.m. on 15 December 2007 against the USA at the London Irish stadium in Sunbury, where they were based at the time. Why anyone thought it was a good idea for England to play home matches at London Irish one season and London Welsh the next was beyond me, but we did! London Welsh were not good hosts in my opinion, but the Sunbury hospitality and the welcome at London Irish was great. For me it felt extra-special to be captaining my first England game at the ground where I had received my first ever rugby certificate after taking part in a rugby festival there with Folkestone minis back in 1990. And to add to this special feeling, the current Folkestone girls' team played a curtain-raiser match against London Irish before the game. Looking over to the touchlines and seeing lots of green shirts from Folkestone was fantastic. An adult ticket to our game cost a whole £3! I remember a season later the players were involved in a discussion about raising the ticket price for women's games. I wholeheartedly agreed; we needed to assert our value and selling tickets for £3 did not do this.

The lead-up to the game was not great for me. I was in the gym at Bath just a couple of weeks before, completing a weights session. I was doing a lift called clean and jerk, which involved lifting a bar and weights up to my chin then pushing them up above my head. Whilst doing this something went in my back and all I could do was collapse on the floor. Sophie Hemming was in the main hall along with our strength-and-conditioning trainer and somehow I managed to get myself off the floor and along to the hall where I promptly just lay back down on the ground again. They called for a physio, but there was not much that could be done at that point. My back had gone into complete muscle spasm and until the spasm reduced they could not investigate further. I was lying flat on my back for several days before my first training camp as captain, just a week before our USA game. I managed to get to the training camp a few days later, driven by Sophie, but took no active part. This felt like a huge backward step when I wanted to do my best to present myself as a strong new leader. As someone who, at the time, knew only how to lead by example, this was tough. This added to my self-belief worries and feelings that I was a fraud.

A few days later and I still did not know if I would be able to play in the USA game, but the medics at Bath worked their magic and I was declared fit a couple of days before the game. Amazingly I had not done anything wrong to my back other than the severe muscle spasms I experienced. My back has never been good since and I suffer from fairly regular pain. It has been suggested to me that I would be wise not to get a scan now though for fear of what they might find. Fellow former rugby players will understand this! We won that first game against USA and my captaincy got off to a good start in terms of on-pitch performances. We won the 2008 Six Nations with a Grand Slam, the 2008 European championships and the 2008 Nations Cup. I had a 100 per cent record so far but this, sadly, was not to remain the case.

In 2009 we lost to Wales in the Six Nations. This was the first time England Women had ever lost to Wales in a history of twenty-two years of playing each other. It felt like it was my fault as captain. I did not make great decisions on the pitch, but one decision in particular still haunts me. We were awarded a penalty kick and I asked Katy Mclean – our kicker and as it happens vice-captain at the time – to kick for goal. Katy refused and kicked for touch instead. I wish I had been more assertive. We lost the game by 1 point – 16 points to 15. Non Evans of Wales ironically kicked a successful penalty at eighty minutes in the final play of the game to win the match. I will never forget Wales's reaction at the end. They were ecstatic and to be honest looked more excited than the Black Ferns did when they won the World Cup. It was sickening to watch. What that game did do, however, was force us to look at our decision-making, particularly with regard to kicking. We agreed a zone around the posts. Within that zone I would make the decision; outside of that zone Katy or whoever was kicking would make the decision about whether they were feeling confident enough to go for posts.

Following that Welsh defeat we beat Ireland in our next game. We picked ourselves up really well and got ourselves back on track. Our video analyst used to spend hours (often when he should have been sleeping) putting videos together for us that we would watch just before we boarded the coach on match day. The videos would be set to music and before the Ireland match he chose well, really well. The song that was selected was 'Ali in the Jungle' by the Hours. Their words have resonated then and continue to do so. Please do look the lyrics up, read them, play the song. The words will stick with you too, I am sure. It is a song about getting knocked down but getting back up again. It is a song about the importance of where you are going, not necessarily about where you are now. It is a song of resilience.

We won that Six Nations championship and it meant more to me at the time than any other of my six tournament wins. Of the six, it was the only one that was not a Grand Slam. It meant so much because we nearly lost it. Nearly losing something really does help to make you understand whether you really want it.

Following the Six Nations we went into what was going to be a really tough summer period for me as captain. I came out of the tournament a stronger leader in some respects, having learned some lessons the tough way. I knew that my communication on the pitch needed to be improved, as did my assertion at times when we were under pressure such as in the Wales game. But I was not feeling like I deserved my title as captain yet. In my own eyes I was still a fraud, an imposter, but, crucially, I knew that I wanted the job. I knew that if I wasn't a true captain yet, one day I would be. I would develop my captaincy as I had developed as an international number 8, but I still had to get through the toughest of times, and my captaincy was being questioned not just by me.

I knew that there was one player who did not like Streety's choice to make me captain. I am not going to name her; that is not what this is about. Apart from speaking to the coaches about my credibility both as captain and as number 8 for England she also started to speak to other players and build a feeling and movement that I should not be captain because I was not good enough. At the same time, I had requested a short amount of time off to attend a Tag Rugby

Trust trip to Uganda. I needed some time out, but I was also desperate to actively volunteer with TRT whilst I was still playing rather than waiting until retirement. (You will understand why TRT was and still is so dear to me later in this book.) I was granted the time off, but it meant that I missed a four-day training camp. This allowed more time for players to start talking behind my back, questioning my captaincy. I came back to a heightened awareness of this after Graham Smith also piled the pressure on. He knew what he was doing – he was testing me and pushing me, knowing that I would come through it stronger. He was doing what was right for the team at the time.

After some time to think, by the summer training camp a couple of weeks later I knew without any doubt that I wanted to continue to be the England captain. I invited a group of senior players together. The group included the player who, I knew, was chief advocate to get the captaincy taken away from me. I placed chairs in a small circle and waited for the group to arrive. I still remember how I was feeling. Nervous, determined, anxious but also confident. Confident because I knew that I could do the job well but also confident because I knew that my passion to be a leader had been ignited. Being captain, I realised, was becoming as special to me as the 8 shirt. I told the group that I was going to continue as captain, that I knew I could do the job, and I laid my emotions out before them. I was passionate about it and I would do the best job I possibly could. After that incredibly tough meeting and tough summer for me there was a new-found respect for me as a leader. I remember Rocky telling me how important that meeting was, that they needed to hear my passion and desire to do the job and that their respect increased because I had laid my emotions bare. I was vulnerable at that time but it strengthened me. The fragility of my captaincy disappeared.

Sometimes following a physical injury, athletes will come back stronger; they have been broken in some way and need to rehabilitate effectively to get back to fitness, but this is often accompanied by a strong resolve and an increased motivation. They now completely understand their desire to keep hold of something that they nearly lost. I experienced a stronger resolve and motivation to play for England after my injury early on in my career in 2004. Without that injury I have no doubt that I would not have become the player and consequently the captain that I was. The emotional struggle and mental pressure I went through regarding my captaincy were no different. I didn't have many injuries when I was playing, but this captaincy struggle (along with my knee injury) was my most significant challenge. I was without doubt stronger afterwards.

A few months later, in the autumn of 2009, New Zealand toured England, and all eyes were on the two teams leading up to the 2010 World Cup. The first game was played at Esher in very windy, blustery conditions. We lost 16-3. This was a bigger margin than our previous game against them in 2006, but we knew that we could beat them nonetheless. We made a few mistakes, missed a couple of tackles and were, we would all agree, far from our best. Gregory once again eloquently describes both the context and the game:

As a geography teacher I will often teach my pupils that the responses after a storm can be short term and long term. England Women played NZ Women in a storm yesterday evening and will be waking up this morning considering their own responses. In the short term they have next week's return test at Twickenham to reverse the result. In the long term they will have the World Cup in nine months' time to think about and develop error-free rugby.

England lost but the result was closer than the 16-3 score-line. New Zealand scored the softest of tries at international level and England will be rueing a couple of missed opportunities. It could so easily have been England Women waking with the smiles of victory on their lips.

Before kick-off the comparisons between the last two games of these two sides were uncannily similar. The weather was awful just as it was in 2006 at the World Cup final where, despite the conditions, the two sides served up what could arguably be described as the greatest women's game ever. But three years is a long time in international rugby and as I sat nervously waiting for the game to start I wondered what this game would produce.

The women's counterparts playing at Twickenham yesterday have had well publicised injury woes but so too have these women. Rochelle Clark, the talismanic prop, was injured last week. Sarah Hunter, the excellent blindside, is out. Danielle Waterman, one of the game's most dangerous runners, is out with a serious knee injury. It requires full reconstruction and an estimated twelve months' recovery but with characteristic grit Nolli is determined to be fighting fit and pulling a shirt on in nine months' time at the World Cup.

But with the withdrawals so too come the returnees. Tamara Taylor takes her place on the bench and will be looking forward to reuniting her second-row partnership with Jo McGilchrist. Maggie Alphonsi makes her return to the starting line-up. I never tire of watching this remarkable athlete play. To my mind she is the best player of the game, man or woman, full stop.

And what of New Zealand? It's easy to say they will be good. No, easy to say they will be very good, but just how very good they will be is more tricky to say. They play such few internationals it is difficult to know where their weaknesses could be, but more ominously it is even more difficult to know what their strengths may be.

The opening exchanges of this game were looking positive for England. Alice Richardson found a half gap in the NZ midfield and put in a nice offload. NZ gave away a penalty but then touch was not made by England. The wind was howling down the pitch and this was to hamper England's ability to make yards with their kicking game. New Zealand, with the wind right behind them, just had to tap the ball to make fifty yards.

But England were finding gaps and Spence made a telling break from the scrum and fed well to blindside Heather Fisher who stormed down the pitch. Fisher took a break from the sport to have a go at bobsleigh but has since returned with renewed confidence from the Sevens circuit and is now enjoying a renaissance. She had an excellent game and her pace worried the NZ defence. However, after this first break she then handled the ball to give away a penalty. There were far too many of these silly penalties from England which allowed NZ to easily relieve any pressure that England had built up. On fourteen minutes one of these penalties allowed NZ to take a 3-nil lead.

Sophie Hemming, the quietly unassuming prop from Bristol, allowed her rugby to do the talking today. She had a really good game and helped England gain dominance in the scrums. On twenty minutes NZ's scrum was destroyed by the England pack. This allowed a great attacking platform for England and Spence duly obliged with another great break from the back of the scrum linking well with Fisher once more. Fisher was denied a try by an excellent tackle from the NZ fullback. England recycled the ball and England's fullback Charlotte Barras took a great line, but once more excellent defence by New Zealand prevented a score.

But England were still spoiling the pressure they had by giving away penalties which allowed NZ to break out and on twenty-eight minutes NZ scored again to make it 6-nil. New Zealand, though, were also giving away some penalties and the NZ 7 finally had to go. She had already been spoken to for fighting and then stamping and another infringement meant she had to spend ten minutes in the bin. Six minutes later the New Zealand number 8 put in a highly dangerous high tackle on Becky Essex and she might consider herself lucky it was just ten minutes she spent off the pitch. England now had to score and duly pressured the NZ line. England MUST score but they miss a huge overlap and go the wrong way. NZ clear their lines and within the blinking of an eye find themselves with a lineout on England's five-metre line. Last play of the half and England allow the NZ 12 to walk in for the softest of tries at this level. Half time 13-nil to NZ.

England came out in the second half with the wind, which seemed to have eased, but they had players in the bin and they continued to give silly pressure-relieving penalties away. On forty-seven minutes, with New Zealand back to full strength, they went 16-nil up.

England were doing good things but they were still letting themselves down with some poor options. These poor options were a sixteenth defender for NZ and these will have to be eliminated for next week. At fifty-eight minutes England finally get on the scoreboard with a penalty but it has taken longer than it needed to.

And this is how it remained till the final whistle. 16-3 to NZ.

New Zealand probably just deserved to edge this game courtesy of their defence when it mattered, but 13 points is not a clear reflection of the two teams. England could have won this game and the video analysis will highlight a need to get rid of silly penalties and a need to pressure NZ for longer periods. England manged to panic New Zealand's defence on their line on a couple of occasions but will need to do this more consistently to get the win next week.

But it must be remembered you do not have a close game with New Zealand if you have played poorly and England's players can reflect on some very good performances. Sophie Hemming was strong in the scrum and effective in the loose. Fisher covered lots of ground and was always a threat with ball in hand. Spence was strong as ever and sharp off the scrum and Maggie Alphonsi, with some massive pile-driver-type tackles, was, as expected, a thorn in New Zealand's side. The men's game at Twickenham next week has now become a curtain raiser. The clash between the women is mouth-watering. It promises to be massive.

Credit crunch? The entrance to the women's game is free. Absolute bargain. It should be a golden game.

They were down to thirteen players and they scored before half-time. I said in my post-match interview that we panicked and tried too hard in that period. How could I have helped as captain? Should we have been more direct in where we focused our attack, or should we have continued as normal without adding psychological pressure that we had to score while they were short of their full complement? Ultimately what lost us this game was giving away too many penalties (not something we were really known for) and missing opportunities. New Zealand did not win that day because they were fantastic, they won because we were not.

After the game we knew that we could and should play better and that if we did we knew without doubt that we could beat the Black Ferns. That game, although we lost, proved to us that they were not invincible. This loss also almost perfectly set up what was to come. It made what happened next even more special.

Chapter Ten

The Leader in Me

The second test was at Twickenham. Our warm-up time out on the pitch kept being reduced. There was a delay with the men's match, I believe because the referee got injured, which meant that the majority of our warm-up was in the confines of the changing room, and I loved it. We were so close together, swapping over on bikes and rowing machines. When we did get out on the pitch we only had fifteen minutes of warm-up left. I loved this too, as it meant that we had to be completely focused on what we were doing, completely switched on and attuned to us and only us. I loved captaining that game. I had a number of good breaks from the scrum, which the Ferns struggled to contain. Claire Purdy (prop) made a fantastic break down the wing and the ball found its way over to me to score the only try of the game. Gill Burns was on commentary and awarded me the Player of the Match award. Maybe it was number 8 loyalty, but maybe I did deserve it. Either way, thank you, Burnsie. Graham Smith wrote in an email to me some years later, when reflecting back on my captaincy and the summer of 2009, that 'the challenges that you had to overcome resulted in your best performance for England v New Zealand at Twickenham in 2009 on the occasion of your 50 cap'. I definitely turned another corner on this day with my captaincy. Something clicked and I realised that day that, yes, I was a leader and, yes, I was a good one to boot.

Gregory had this to say about the match:

Twenty-four hours ago exactly, at 5:06 p.m. England Women's game against the reigning World Champions was twenty-one minutes old. What happened over the next minute highlights why England have every chance of lifting the World Cup in nine months' time.

On twenty-one minutes New Zealand gave away a penalty. Katy Mclean then made good ground with her touch finder. England found themselves on the halfway line. A well-worked shortened line-out move from England sets Catherine Spencer driving up field. The ball is spun wide, and with Maggie Alphonsi a decoy runner, Claire Purdy finds herself with space and makes twenty cracking metres. Kat Merchant continues this and makes more ground deep into the Kiwi 22. The ball is then recycled back across and Heather Fisher comes agonisingly close to breaking through to score. Again, England maintain continuity, and more importantly maintain pressure on the New Zealand defence. The ball comes right and Mclean feeds Catherine Spencer who ghosts past the Kiwi 12 to touch down for an excellent try.

There was so much in this try for England to be proud of. The well-worked line-out and forward dominance, the skill level in the passing, the development of players such as Purdy who has stepped up to the mark in Rochelle Clark's absence, the continuity and lack of panic, the clinical finish. This was England at their best. If they could play this error-free exhibition rugby for eighty minutes then no side would come in touching distance.

Despite this it was actually New Zealand who started the better of the two teams. England were doing good things but were also letting themselves down with some sloppy play. An intercept pass followed by a kick charge down almost let New Zealand score within the first five minutes. England's mistakes allowed New Zealand to continue to pressure and at twelve minutes the New Zealand fly-half hit a good drop goal. England were, once again, like last week, gaining superiority in the scrum and Spencer made some good drives off the back of the scrum supported by the ever-present Maggie Alphonsi. But, like last week, England found it hard to go more than a few phases without an error. Last week England allowed this self-inflicted pressure to lead to a try for New Zealand. This week, however, the defence stood firm and Katy Mclean, who had a point to prove, made a good number of important tackles throughout the match.

At half-time England found themselves leading at 7-3. The crowd was confident of a victory but New Zealand had started to form a good driving maul and their big and dangerous backs will slip through the smallest of holes in any defence. England know they must play some phases and create pressure and ensure their defence is entirely watertight. And, answering the crowd's pleas, from the off England came out firing. Alphonsi and Hemming put in a combo super hit and force a turnover. England maintain that pressure and Mclean slots a drop goal to make it 10-3 to England.

At fifty minutes England threaten New Zealand's line for perhaps the last time in the match. Kat Merchant makes a superb break out of her 22 and heads towards the NZ ten-metre line. She holds the ball up well and it is recycled where Alphonsi makes a good bust up midfield. Once more good recycling from England's forwards, who now have the fresh legs of Tamara Taylor, and the ball is spun to Heather Fisher who shows all her 7s pace to be held up just short of the line for the second time in the game.

This last half hour of the game tested England's character. A couple of times New Zealand were awarded penalty kicks but where in the wind of Esher the NZ fly-half slotted her kicks, here in the downpour of Twickenham her kicking boots were found wanting. New Zealand had all the territory in this last quarter of the game but time and again the England girls stood up when it counted. Tackles were made and turnovers won but England could not convert this belligerence into any form of sustained pressure. At the final whistle the delight on the girls' faces was obvious and the relief and joy amongst supporters abundant.

Despite the torrents of rain this was a wonderful advert for the women's game. The dull adjectives and negative commentary that shrouds the men's game at the moment were not evident at all. Both sides were not afraid to run and play rugby and the heart and spirit coupled with skill and finesse is something the men could and should learn from.

Taking the game in isolation this was a wonderful victory for England's women. Credit must go to New Zealand for their never-say-die attitude but England should be allowed to enjoy this victory between two very good sides. Between now and the World Cup England have the Six Nations tournament and they will be looking to build on their success here and continue to develop powerful, skilful, clinical rugby. But England know, as do the rest of the rugby-playing world, that New Zealand will be smarting from this loss. The New Zealand women do not suffer from the World Cup yips that their male counterparts do and the Black Ferns will be hoping to deliver a Black Storm in south-west London next August.

Gregory's last words in this write-up were so true. That storm, as we now know, did return. We were strong enough to thwart it – and yet we did not.

We gained a lot of media profile following this 2009 victory – only the second ever against the mighty Black Ferns and the first since 2001. Even Des Lynam (again, if you are too young to know who he is, Google him!) saw fit to mention it in his round-up of the weekend's TV sporting action for the *Daily Telegraph*. And most mainstream print and online media featured our momentous victory, understanding the significance of such a win nine months away from the World Cup. For me personally, that day really was up there as one of my top rugby-playing highlights. Gary Street once again offered his comments to the media after the game.

It's brilliant to win here at Twickenham in front of our biggest ever crowd . . . We won this game because of our physicality; our defence was tremendous and we really believed in ourselves. Catherine Spencer today put on one of the great Twickenham performances. To come out and play as well as she did, being captain and earning her fiftieth cap is amazing. She is a tremendous athlete and brilliant leader of this team.

These were amazing words from Streety, and whilst my great Twickenham performance will be very low on the pecking order due to my gender, to me it will always remain hugely significant and impactful because of my ability to lead that day.

That evening Amy Garnett came up to me and said three words: 'Well led today.' I will never forget it and I know that she would not have said this lightly. Garnett was a lady of few words and although she was not the ringleader in the move to remove the captaincy from me I know that she was enlisted to the cause early on. But she meant what she said and that was huge for me. That day, more than two years after the phone call I initially made to Streety whilst sitting in my little Micra on my lunch break, was when I really became England captain. That was the day when I realised I was not acting any more, when I realised that I was a leader.

As amazing as the 2009 victory was, as much as I was enjoying my personal achievements, this victory nine months out from the World Cup was the worst thing that could have happened to us. New Zealand had renewed motivation to turn things round before August 2010.

Although I got to the stage where I felt I was a good and successful leader (despite the 2010 loss) it is difficult for captains to know when we are doing a good job. It is hard to analyse captaincy as we might do other aspects of our game. It is easy to measure how many tackles or offloads we made, how many breakdowns we made an impact at or the success percentage of the set piece. Rugby, although emotionally driven, is pretty 'SMART'. We can set targets and analyse performance as we might do in a business environment. We can set Specific, Measurable, Attainable, Relevant and Timely goals which are nicely wrapped up in player feedback forms or business appraisals. The same cannot be said of leadership. Leadership is not SMART. The actions of leadership can be – for example making time to speak with members of your team – but leadership itself is not. So how do we know? We need to look for the signs.

During the 2009 Nations Cup in Canada our awesome and incredible manager Janette 'Jan Man' Shaw had to take a break from the tour to fly home to attend a funeral. This coincided with the easier game of the tour, against South Africa. The decision was made that I would be rested for the game and take over as squad manager for the time that Jan Man was away. Charlotte 'Beanie' Barras, otherwise known as Charlotte Banana due to a slightly dyslexic stadium announcer at the 2006 World Cup, would take over as captain. For the first day or so after Jan Man was away I pretty much took on the manager's role in addition to the captaincy, but from shirt presentation the evening before the South Africa match until after the game Beanie was England captain. Following the game, which England won, Beanie spoke to me and said that she could not wait to hand the captaincy, back. She had had no idea how much work was required and she was shattered. She could not believe it was such a tough job. For two reasons this pleased me. Firstly, it was good that the players did not know how tough captaincy was. It is a profile role because you get to lift trophies and speak to the media and so on and you are the main spokesperson and figurehead for the team and wider sport, but most of the job has to go unseen. We are a filter of information, a shield for our team mates and a workhorse – getting jobs done so that our team mates can go out and give their best performance. All this whilst still doing our own day job of trying to be the best in our position to ensure our continued selection. Captaincy does not guarantee selection. I was also pleased because this seemingly casual, slightly jokey comment from Beanie told me that I was doing a good job. That I was getting on with something that was difficult and a challenge, but I was doing it.

Later on in that tour in Canada we were on the coach heading somewhere. I didn't know where we were but Heather Fisher called up the bus to ask me how long it would take till we got to our destination, a bit like a child asking a parent because they know everything. I replied 'ten minutes', not knowing at all, but my answer satisfied her for a while. For me this little question was another sign that I was on the right track – that I was starting to be acknowledged as a leader.

Following retirement, I was still aware of signs that I was a good captain and that I was continuing to be a leader. Kim Oliver, who I trained alongside at Bath University for many years, was having a party to celebrate her thirtieth birthday. Kim was a fantastic player but her career was cut far too short by ongoing problems with her knee. Now head coach of Bristol Bears in the women's premiership, she is making an impact once again. Georgie Rozario (now Gulliver) organised much of the party and a good number of former England team mates attended. Amongst them were Sarah Hunter and Katy Mclean, two more recent England captains, but as soon as we got together in that group I became the leader and decision-maker again. The decisions were not quite so impactful in life as on the pitch, but it was still important to make sure that everyone was in a taxi at the end of the night to head back to the rugby club near Bath where we were camping!

I learned some key lessons during my time as captain and, as simple as they sound, they helped me immensely:

- You can't please everyone all of the time
- Make decisions – not everything should be shared/discussed
- Use the strength of others
- These things help you to be authentic

There are so many theories about leadership, what leadership is and so on. The main thing that connects them seems to be that everyone is different. We may be born with some predisposed leadership traits or we may develop them. We might have to borrow behaviours at some times and we will vary our style depending on the situation. Sometimes we will be more laissez-faire, other times more autocratic. I don't think that we can succinctly say what good or bad leadership is because there are so many different situations that require leadership and it annoys me when people try to put leadership into nicely packaged corporate workshops. I do deliver leadership workshops through Inspiring Women, I will admit, but my focus is on recognising ourselves as leaders and understanding that everyone will need to be a leader at some point in their life. We don't need a team of a hundred people to manage in order to describe ourselves as a leader. I also look in more detail at female traits that might hold us back from developing our own leadership. I use a very simple technique involving bright pink Post-it notes that demonstrates very clearly how much we apologise or put ourselves down as women in our normal everyday conversations. My leadership workshops do not try to fit everyone into one leadership style or box. In the same way that I do when I talk to primary-school children, I simply ask people to look up, look around and look forward.

When I think back to my captaincy days, the one area of leadership that meant more to me than any other was instilling confidence in other players: creating an environment that new players could come into, feel welcomed, feel valued and most importantly not feel like a fraud: making them feel that they belonged. I received the following message from a player when I retired, and her words not only meant a huge amount to me but also sum up what I think is important about leadership:

You were England captain when I earned my first cap in 2008 in Scotland in the Six Nations and yes of course I was 'shitting a brick' – inevitably. I clearly remember your facial expression when you spoke and presented me with my cap. I felt belief, pride and trust and it was a perfect introduction to the senior squad. You made me feel like I belonged to the team and really just made the occasion extra-special. I wasn't embarrassed to get up like I normally would be – everything just felt calm. I have you to thank for that.

You have brought professionalism, strong leadership and a fantastically calming influence to my time within the squad – captain or not. You are undeniably a world-class player, but above all you evoke a feeling of pride and teamship that no one can match. You will be missed, but never forgotten.

Many people think of Churchillian speeches and moments of public leadership when they think of what makes a good captain, but to me without a doubt the most important aspect is the individual relationship with team members: to ensure that they understand the new world around them and feel equipped to be part of it; to inspire someone, to be a shoulder when needed, to be a confidante, a source of knowledge, a reassurance. All of these very private moments equal good and strong leadership. I didn't know what good leadership was when I first took over the captaincy armband, but I do now and I am thankful for that.

Chapter Eleven
The Toughest Challenge

To this date, I don't really know how or why I made the decision to retire. I also still don't know if it was the right thing to do. Quite possibly until the day I die will never know if I made the right choice, nor will I be able to manage my emotions to accept that my decision was 100 per cent correct. What I do know with certainty, however, is that retirement from international rugby has without doubt been the toughest challenge of my sports career.

My ascent to playing for England and then becoming England captain was of a gradual nature, but the end of my career was swift in comparison. I had no idea in February 2011 what retirement would be like; if I had any idea I am certain that I would have carried on for longer, playing my beloved sport in the international playing world that was so familiar and comfortable for me at the time.

I made the decision before the 2010 World Cup that I would not even think about retiring at that point. My mind was starting at times to think about life beyond rugby and I was starting to ask myself when the best time to make that change would be, but I put these thoughts out of my head for the immediate future. Regardless of our result I knew that it would be an emotional and mentally tough time; adding any decision about retirement then would not be the right thing for me to do. Whether we won or lost I knew that I would carry on for another season, but I was pretty certain before 2010 that I would not carry on until 2014. Why not? Now it is something that plagues me. If I was fit and healthy why did I not carry on, why did I not give every ounce of myself to continuing on my quest to win a World Cup? Why did I step down in 2011 when my peers such as Rocky Clark, Maggie Alphonsi and Tamara Taylor carried on? I have always explained that I retired because I wanted to make the decision on my terms, that I didn't want to be de-selected or forced to retire through injury; I thought it would be easier to make the decision myself. Now, having met and spoken to many retired athletes from a broad range of sports, I know that retiring on your own terms is tremendously tough. At the other end of the retirement scale, being forced to retire through injury is, I am sure, really hard, but it is a decision that is made for you; there is no choice. There will be anger and hurt against an external situation or person but surely this will not be aimed at yourself.

How do I deal with the choice that I made? The decision to shatter my own dream? To not give everything to win the World Cup? I have no person or situation to direct my anger towards other than myself. Why did I retire? How do I come to terms with my decision and accept that without question it was the right thing to do? I have to somehow reach this conclusion because if I don't I am never going to be completely happy. I will never make peace.

The first rung on my ladder to the end was making the decision to step down from the captaincy. I took over the role at the start of the 2007 season and carried on until after the 2010 World Cup, but prior to the 2011 Six Nations I remember thinking that I wanted to play without the extra responsibility. I wanted to be selfish for a while and focus on my own game. I don't think that my performance was necessarily affected by the captaincy; however I was not only juggling life as an elite athlete with a full-time job, I was also squeezing in an international captaincy role. Not easy. But looking back now I do wish that I had retained the captaincy until full retirement because I loved being captain; sometimes when you lose something you realise how much you love it.

I have been looking back at some emails recently and I wrote the below to David Flatman in January 2011:

It was a really, really tough decision to step down from the captaincy – I was quite emotional!! Feels a bit like splitting up from someone that you care about a lot but for the right reasons. I will miss the captaincy loads but I just want to focus on myself as a player for a bit and try to reach my potential before I am too old!!

Flats had written a great article in support of women's rugby around the time, highlighting the changes and development of the game triggered by the award to Maggie for World Rugby Player of the Year from the prestigious and highly respected Rugby Union Writers' Club. I had won a recognition award a couple of years earlier, but this award to Maggie, as Flats explained, 'called out that the winds had changed for women's rugby'. People were starting to take note of us as talented rugby players. Flats went on to say (after I bribed him with coffee):

> England's No. 8 Catherine Spencer trains in the same gym as us in Bath and, well, wow. I don't know what time she gets up in the morning but I am pathologically early and have never beaten her to the treadmill. Anyone can get up early, I hear you cry, but does she do any work there? To prove the point, I will quote my good friend Butch James: 'I'm going back to the coffee shop. I ain't squatting till she's gone. It's embarrassing.' Or, I can quote Bath and England tighthead prop Duncan Bell: 'I honestly think she could beat me in a fight.'

On further interrogation of Mr Flatman it transpired that Bell's quote was not completely direct but when suggested he would like to be assigned that quote he said, 'She probably bloody could.' And for Butch James – 100 per cent true quote. To be fair, he was a fly-half.

Flatman's article concluded:

> The likes of Spencer and Alphonsi are strikingly athletic and, when playing, staggeringly good. Spencer is in a similar mould to Nick Easter in that she seems able to carry the ball over the gain line almost at will and seems never to get tired (tone: jealous). Alphonsi, well, she is a machine built for rugby . . . So these are the characters charged with taking their beloved game into uncharted territory. Through grit and diligence,

they seek to gain profile for a sport which for so long has been dismissed by an ignorant majority.

So yes, we were travelling towards uncharted territory, not just acceptance but recognition was building, reward was starting to surface and I was stepping away.

At a training camp prior to the start of the Six Nations in 2011, I told Streety, Graham, Maggie and Katy Mclean of my decision to retire, and remember bursting into tears as I spoke to them. Then, a few days later, I sent out the following email to all of the players:

Dear all

I am emailing to let you all know that I have made the decision to step down from the England captaincy.

This has, without doubt, been one of the hardest decisions that I have ever had to make and it is one that I have been mulling over for quite some time. To captain your country is one of the biggest honours that you can hold and I have decided to give it up – am I completely crazy?! There are many, many reasons why I would dearly love to continue being England Captain though there are also reasons personal to me that have led me to this decision.

One of you reading this will be the next England captain – WOW! Many people dream of playing for their country in their chosen sport, only some of us achieve this. Many people dream of captaining their country, even fewer of us achieve this. You will join a group of a very small number of people who will experience the honour of leading your country. Relish it, enjoy it and be proud of it. I will support you all the way.

From your 'ex' Captain.

Spence

Forcing myself to look at the bigger picture and towards the future, I also felt that it was time for Streety and Graham to look at other leaders – selfless to the end, even when I was doing my best to be selfish. In business terms it was important to ensure sustainability through succession planning. It had taken me at least two years to be comfortable with the captaincy so why not give someone else a head start on their own leadership journey and give them more time to flourish before the next World Cup.

After stepping down from the captaincy my next step was to retire completely from international rugby. The sport I thought I loved. I told Streety and Graham before the beginning of the 2011 Six Nations that I was going to retire at the end of the tournament. I remember that I phoned them both from the same car park I had been parked in when I phoned Streety to first put my hand up for captaincy. It seemed apt. However, I then spent more time on the bench in that Six Nations than I had across my whole England career. Of course, Streety and Graham needed to start looking to the future, but I hated this. I remembered feeling let down by a previous England captain who had sprung her retirement decision on us. She had told us at the end of a match at the side of the pitch following a game at Twickenham a year out from the 2006 World Cup. I didn't want to do that. The team was always the most important thing. I was so lucky throughout my career with regard to selection, with the vast majority of my caps coming from a starting shirt. I was occasionally rested or put on the bench during squad rotation against easier oppositions (I never did get to play Kazakhstan!) so I can't complain too much about only experiencing the challenges of being a bench player during my last Six Nations campaign. Club and country do their best now to market these bench players or substitutes as impact players or game-changers, but every player wants a starting shirt and that will never change.

I did say, from my seat in the Sky Sports studio during the 2014 World Cup, that as a coach I would select my bench first. There is a skill to coming on during the match rather than starting and some players are better suited to it than others. Some players will see a drop of performance when not starting, some will raise their game, utilising an effective release of pent-up energy when they are finally unleashed to the pitch – the modern-day coach has to look at the best combinations. I also think it is important, however, for the whole team to still train to be eighty-minute players. There are some matches that are better suited to fewer changes to the team, and coaches should trust the players on the pitch to start and finish a job. If the player bubble on the pitch seems right, then don't change it just because you feel you should. In today's game, when players are arguably fitter and stronger, it infuriates me that some will never play more than fifty minutes. The use of tactical substitutions is difficult and in my role as director of women's rugby at Old Elthamians (albeit not at the lofty heights of international rugby) or as coach at Aylesford Bulls prior to that I came to understand the challenge. In my opinion Simon Middleton got the tactics completely wrong in the 2017 World Cup final. He made too many changes too soon.

The last ever game my brothers watched me play in an England shirt was against Scotland at Twickenham on 13 March 2011. I did start that game but I was subbed off very shortly into the second half. I understood the reasons – Streety and Graham needed to start playing Sarah Hunter at 8 rather than her usual 6 – but of course I did not want to leave that pitch. I had had no heads-up that it was going to happen either so I was not prepared at all. And worst of all my family were not prepared. We beat Scotland by a cricket score that day and were running tries in for fun, but my dad said afterwards that he and my brothers were the only England supporters looking glum in the second half. My brothers would never watch me play for England again.

Two weeks later I was sub for my last ever game for England – something I found incredibly tough when the 8 shirt meant so much to me. But I did run out with the same number on my back as I did for my first cap – 19 – so in my mind this was kind of OK. The game was against Ireland away. My parents flew out to watch; Mr Nearly Right had also booked to fly out but typically was late leaving work and missed his flight and didn't make it over to Ireland. Well done, him!

I went on about five minutes into the second half. I think I probably had one of the worst games of my career. I was so incredibly conscious that I was experiencing the last moments of my England career and this was meddling with my mind. I was normally so composed and unaffected by external pressures, but not on this day. Agonisingly, there was a giant clock positioned in the corner of the ground, and it seemed that every time I looked up from a scrum, ruck or tackle this clock was there in my direct eyeline. The seconds were ticking down so loudly it was deafening. And when that final whistle blew I just sobbed and I could not stop for quite some time. I could not quite believe that this was actually happening. I very nearly scored a try in that game; I was just centimetres away from the line. It was the only day in my whole career that I wanted to score a try for myself rather than for the team. I was devastated that I didn't. Scoring on my first and last games for England would have wrapped it up nicely. I realise now that I crave a neat packaging for my career; two try-scoring bookends would have helped.

Because it was the last game of the tournament and because it was also the Grand Slam winning game there was a lot of milling around on the pitch at the end, lots of people standing there celebrating. I didn't quite know what to think. This was the last time I would be in this situation: at the end of a rugby game in an England shirt. I spoke to my parents, to a few of the players, I spoke to Streety and Graham, all the while in a state of unreality. It had not hit me. I was emotional of course but I didn't understand then the full gravity of what was happening.

As with the 2010 World Cup game, I don't remember getting changed. I have tried really hard to remember being in the changing room but I can't. The next thing I remember is being in the post-match function room along with the Irish team and various hangers-on.

Before the start of the Six Nations, apart from informing Streety and Graham I also told three close team mates:

Sophie Hemming, Maggie Alphonsi and Claire Purdy (the original 2010 grannies along with Jo McGilchrist, Amy Garnett and myself). Unbeknownst to me they had arranged for some gifts to be presented to me at the end of that game. I wish I had known. My parents were in an adjoining bar – I wish they could have seen the standing ovation I received from everyone in the room: England players and staff and all of the Ireland squad and hangers-on. It was emotional to say the least. But they did not see this, as I had no idea that it was going to happen. After the main formalities were over I went through to the main bar to be with my parents. I don't think they knew what to think. They must have been hurting because they too would never experience quite the same emotions again, watching their baby girl running out and representing her country. My brothers, who could not make it over due to work, would never again give their sister the 'nod' before a game. They would have been grieving too.

My family were always immensely proud and really enjoyed supporting me and the team throughout my career, but my decision had ended that for them. How were they meant to feel? Of course, they could and would continue to support England Women, but never again with the same emotional attachment. I hadn't discussed my decision to retire with them – it was solely a personal decision – but perhaps I should have done? If I had spoken to them, would I have carried on playing? Would I have been part of that 2014 World Cup winning squad? We never really talked about retirement in general and the challenges of this, so I didn't fully understand what feelings they were experiencing, and they didn't fully understand mine. Looking back, it would have been really, really good to chat more with my family. But I didn't. I was Catherine Spencer; I was strong and independent. But I now feel that I owed them some input into my decision. They had been on my journey with me, emotionally and physically, and had invested so much. I am sure that it hurt them that I retired without ever giving them any option to talk through the decision. Was my decision to retire selfish, just as my quest to win a World Cup was? Am I selfish person?

I had told the team of my decision to retire at our shirt-presentation ceremony on the night before that last game, at our team hotel in Ireland. I'd asked our manager Jan Man if I could speak to the players personally. We started proceedings as normal. The squad were sitting down and our management team were standing at the front. Messages were given out along with any other details we needed prior to the next day. I purposely sat on the front row so that the team could not see my tears. Then Jan Man invited me to speak. I stood up and could hardly get the words out. The room itself was quite large but we were tucked into a corner, creating our own special bubble, and I felt the space close in even further as I tried to convey to the team what I was thinking. I didn't want to make the moment about me – we had a squad job to do the next day – but I did want the chance to tell them that it would be my last game. I remember seeing some quite shocked faces. My announcement came as a surprise and as I was speaking it felt like someone else's voice. At the time I was already questioning what I was doing. I was in shock that it was actually happening, but for the first time, as I listened to that voice – my voice – my decision felt real. As the words were coming out of my mouth, loud enough for all to hear, it was as if this was the first time I was hearing those words too: 'This will be my last ever game for England.' There was so much of me at the time that wanted to stop what I was saying, apologise for making a mistake, sit down and carry on with shirt presentation as normal and announce that I would not be retiring after all. But of course I could not do that. I had made my decision, right or wrong, so I had to stick with it. It felt like the decision was now out of my control. Should I have taken back control? Could I have done?

After the game, a press release was issued announcing my retirement and there followed a flurry of supporting words and thank-yous.

Publicly, rugby correspondent for *The Times* and *Sunday Times* Stephen Jones said, 'You did an absolutely wonderful job for women's rugby and for rugby in general the past few weeks and years. Many congratulations for the way you carried yourself on and off the field.' And in an email direct to me: 'I know what a major decision it would have been for you to announce your retirement. Do I know you well enough to be cheeky? Hope so. All I hope is that this is really what you want and that no other person or non-selection pushed you towards it. You clearly have a good few more years left if you wanted them.' Yes Steve, you do know me well enough to ask that question. And no, I was not pushed, it was entirely my decision, but I cannot say that it was what I really wanted. Steve went on to say: 'If you are dead set on retiring then I wish you all the best for the future. I put you alongside Gill Burns for what you did for women's rugby on and off the field, and very many congratulations.' This message, along with those I received from team mates, has stuck with me. Burnsie is the highest of the high in my opinion. A phenomenal leader, player, ambassador, influencer ... the list of her attributes goes on. For someone as highly regarded as Stephen Jones to write that means so much.

There were stacks of messages from people I didn't even know received by the RFU through social-media outlets. Here are just a few:

'Great career Cath Spencer, you have honoured the English flag, thank you.'

'Well done, great player and role model. England will miss her loads.'

'Thanks for all the hard work Cath – you've been a world-class leader and a superb role model within the game and outside of it, and a brilliant player in your own right ... Your boots will be very difficult to fill.'

'I have had the pleasure of refereeing you on a number of occasions, most recently against Saracens ladies. Assuming you were not the guilty party that sent me sprawling with a shove from behind, I would like to wish you all the best in your retirement. You are a class act as a player and have been a great role model to the ladies game at club and national level.'

I don't specifically remember that Saracens game but if

the referee was in the way I can't deny that it may have been me!

'Come on England this girl deserves a gong.'
'Should be in the Birthday Honours list after a career like that.'

A handful of the England players have now received recognition via the honours system. The men's team, after their 2003 World Cup victory, all received MBEs, but in a move of great inequality the women were not all awarded MBE's after their World Cup victory in 2014. I was never nominated and have consequently never received this kind of recognition. I would like to receive notification – not so that I could add some letters after my name or go to a nice ceremony in London and meet royalty, but so that I could turn it down. I am not belittling anyone who has received such honours, as many of them deserve recognition in some form; it is the concept of honouring the past system of the British Empire that I struggle with. I also think it is completely unjust and unfair that the 2014 winning squad were not offered the same recognition as the men; then there is the fact that the nomination process seems to have become a business. Organisations make good money drawing up nominations for those that can afford to pay. This does not seem right at all. So for these three reasons I would turn it down if it ever came my way – which seems highly unlikely now, I would think, and even more so having just written this! In a similar vein I never sang the national anthem before matches. This did not mean that I was any less proud to play for my country. On the contrary, it was a huge honour. I just didn't feel it necessary to sing to the Queen beforehand. I am sure that she is a lovely lady, but that is not why I spent hours and hours in the gym or on the pitch. And lastly the national anthem is British. I would love to see England take on an anthem that can be sung with as much pride as 'Land of my Fathers' or 'Flower of Scotland' or 'Ireland's Call' . . . Now those I do quietly sing along to!

The messages continued to trickle in:

'Hire her to take over Johnno. Sure she'll do a better job . . .'

(No comment)

'She was an amazing player and captain. A fantastic role model for women's rugby. I'm glad that I got to meet her a few times and see her play, on the TV and in person.'

Gary Street offered his quote to the official press release on my retirement:

Catherine is one of the great players in the modern era whose physical presence dominated many games. She captained my first game in charge for England and developed her captaincy skills culminating in an outstanding effort, on and off the pitch, during the World Cup. One of her finest days was winning her fiftieth cap at Twickenham, leading the side in our defeat of New Zealand and scoring an unforgettable try. Her tireless work off the field has helped develop the profile of the women's game and she will continue to do this in her working role within the RFUW. Her cool demeanour disguises her beating rugby heart and she will be truly missed.

I love this last sentence from Streety, it summed me up so well at the time. My heart did beat for rugby, from the moment I woke up to the moment I closed my eyes at night. But this did not often show outwardly because of my calm nature; the disguising of my emotions is something that went with me into retirement. Not always for the best. My emotions spilled over at times but more often than not they were locked away. Looking back, I should have shown my emotions a little more in the first couple of years as captain; if the players could have seen how much it all meant to me it would have made my job easier. It took a while for them to understand this, along with one very tough summer as I explained in Chapter Nine.

When I came to retire the players did understand me and did recognise what playing for England and the captaincy meant to me. For my retirement Maggie Alphonsi organised for the players to write personal messages to me in an album. Maggie and I were roomies and had a really close bond throughout our careers and this was a lovely thing for her to arrange. I still have the album, of course, but the words written there are going to remain within the covers. Some things should not be shared and for me those words are some of them, but I cry every time I read them. I cry because I retired knowing that the players did get me and had a wealth of respect and care for me that I did not fully understand before reading their words. One overriding theme was the thanks for my support and nurturing of new players. This is something that I am very proud of, helping new players to feel confident and flourish from their first cap onwards. The second overriding theme was understanding my passion to be an ambassador for the game, especially as captain. In recent times my passion for helping to develop the game, and therefore call out things that are not going so well, has often been received defensively by some at the RFU. I am no longer an ambassador or spokesperson for the RFU, but I have been an ambassador for the game in general. Sometimes it feels like there is a world of difference between the two.

The thing about announcing your retirement is that for a few days and weeks, while the lovely messages are coming in, you feel quite good about yourself. If you are ever in need of a confidence boost or to be reminded that you are good at something then I recommend it; but after the high of personal gratification comes the low. The emptiness, the loneliness. Then the questioning. Did I do the right thing? If the answer is no, it is too late, because some decisions cannot be changed. I have never understood those people who announce their retirement amongst a flood of supporting messages, showered with gifts and testimonial dinners and so on, only to seemingly forget all of this and return to the pitch several months later. International retirement is, for me, a once-in-a-lifetime decision.

Chapter Twelve

The Loosening Grip

As with the aftermath of the 2010 World Cup, I realise now that I needed time after I retired to grieve and to deal with what had happened. But again I was still working at the RFU, I was still playing club rugby, I was still living and breathing rugby. I was still Catherine Spencer, England Captain, and could not get away from it. Did I really want to though? I carried on working for the RFU for another three years, using my profile every day in the game to try to help me spread the word that women and girls can and do play rugby. But whilst this was good for the game, this was not good for me. I was becoming more down about my life; I felt I had no personal identity. After twenty years of looking up, aiming to get to the next stage in my rugby career, for the first time I found myself constantly looking back. Looking back at what I had been, looking back at what we could have achieved if things had been different. I was starting to think that there must be something more, hoping that there *was* something more.

*

My job at the RFU was not hugely well paid but it did provide me with a company car, a monthly pay cheque and the associated security of a pension, sick pay and annual leave and so on. Nevertheless, I was starting to think that I didn't just want to leave the RFU – I needed to. It had ground me down. I didn't have the required energy to fight the constant battles any more. But I also wanted to be me again. I wanted to achieve. I wanted to feel important again and I didn't want to just be ordinary. At the same time, I was attending a lot of events and dinners and consequently listening to a lot of after-dinner speakers. Some were good, some not so good. Overwhelmingly they were all male. I don't have anything against men – quite the opposite, as I have explained, I very much like men – however I knew that there were many women who also had amazing stories to tell but were not given the chance to speak up. I wanted to set up a platform to allow this to happen, which I eventually did, setting up my own speaker agency: Inspiring Women. Moving away from the RFU, doing something different and continuing to be different helped me in the medium term, but my retirement challenges continued.

Back on the rugby pitch I was not completely done. I didn't think that I could hang up my boots for good; I could not go cold turkey, nor did I want to. International retirement was one thing but never experiencing the joy of being in the middle of a driving maul, or making a tackle, or breaking from the scrum, or feeling the match build-up in the changing room, or joining in with the adrenaline- and endorphin-driven post-match chatter? I could not take that away from myself completely, so I made the decision to keep playing club rugby, back in Kent, back to my roots.

Folkestone no longer ran a women's team; if it had that is exactly where I would have headed, but instead I went forty minutes up the M20 to a village rugby club called Aylesford. A good number of my former Folkestone team mates were now playing there so it seemed like the natural choice. I was still living in Bristol at the time, but I was due to head back to the south-east to move in with Mr Nearly Right, who was based in Surrey. Only after I had sold my Bristol flat did we agree that we should go our separate ways. If we had decided earlier I have no doubt that I would still be in Bristol now, but then I would not have enjoyed several great years playing for Aylesford: the minnows punching above our weight.

At the time it didn't really feel like anything particularly special that the newly retired former England captain would join the Championship 2 SE team. For me I was just being normal. I loved my first season. We had a good team for that level and at the end of the season we gained promotion. At the end of the following season we gained promotion again, and at the end of the 2012–13 season we found ourselves in a play-off to gain promotion into the premiership. We beat Waterloo in the North v South match in a close game played at Broadstreet in Coventry. I found some extra energy from somewhere in that match to track back and tackle their winger, who was on her way to a near certain try, but emotion and desire can be hugely impactful at times. Following that game, we were then required to have a second play-off against the bottom-placed team in the premiership, and this team was Thurrock. Promotion is really tough in the women's leagues; they are hesitant to relegate more than one team per year from higher leagues, which stacks the odds against teams wanting to climb up. League victory does not guarantee promotion; two play-off games then need to be won. It is tough.

Thurrock had been a long-time rival club of mine, whether playing all those years ago for Folkestone or more recently for Aylesford. The game was being played at Blackheath. Thurrock had managed to recruit Rachael Burford to their ranks and she was playing in their centres that day. We had a really good fly-half that season from NZ. She was not internationally capped but she should have been. Her time and composure on the ball were outstanding, and she was the best fly-half I have ever played with – sorry, Shelley Rae, Karen Andrew and Katy Daley-Mclean. She also had the ability to raise the standard of the players around her, players who mostly lived five minutes away from the village club that we were playing for and who were now on the verge of finding themselves in the top level of English club rugby. Crazy!

We beat Thurrock in a really close game. Despite being such long-time rivals, I really did feel for Thurrock at the end of the game. They were such a passionate and driven team, supported fantastically well by their club, and their pain and hurt at losing was plain to see. Sometimes their passion flowed too much and did not present itself in the best light, but it had to be said that their heart was mostly in the right place.

Meanwhile we had earned promotion to the premiership the hard way: through fifteen years of hard work by the players, some of whom had been team members for almost the whole time. One in particular – Michele Mayhew – was instrumental throughout. Aylesford remained in the premiership for three years, and Gregory and I coached in the third year. That has to be right up there as one of my proudest rugby achievements: keeping that team of local players together for the whole season when we were up against the giants of Saracens, Wasps, Bristol and Richmond. In 2017 Aylesford merged with Harlequins FC to become Harlequins Ladies, a bittersweet time for the game of rugby. Harlequins are now going from strength to strength, breaking records for the number of spectators watching a stand-alone women's match, and have been riding high in the Tyrrell's Premier 15s. But they are only there because of the fight of those local club-rugby women who gained promotion and then retained premiership status. Quite an awesome feat.

At Aylesford, we had to celebrate small battles and victories within games as we were often on the receiving end of some rather large defeats, but the improvement we saw in the team, the level that some of the players reached to play in the premiership, smashing their previously perceived potential, was just awesome. Not one player left because they didn't want to be there any more. Even though we were losing regularly, by celebrating every small victory we were keeping our motivation and our spirits high. Coaching them was a huge challenge but one that both Gregory and I are proud of.

The partnership with Harlequins forged ahead in 2017, which was good for the bigger picture and the development of women's rugby, but it was sad for the village club that for a number of different reasons lost their women's team. Gaining promotion to the premiership was both the best and worst thing to happen to that team. This was another chapter in my rugby journey, not entirely the social rugby I thought it was going to be when I joined at the start of the 2011–12 season but one that I am proud of. But we were a great team on and off the pitch, and like at Folkestone there is still a great connection between the Aylesford players of old.

Outwardly, ever since March 2011, I have said that I retired because I wanted to finish whilst I personally was at the top of my international game. I didn't want to be dropped or get injured. I now struggle with that thought. I was too concerned about what onlookers were thinking. I wanted people to think that I had made the right choice and I thought then that it was important for me to make my own decision. Now how do I feel? I think that I made the wrong decision. My feelings about my failure to win a World Cup are heightened by the knowledge that I gave up. I gave up on my dream. Why did I not give my all? Was I really at the top of my game? I don't think so. I could have got fitter, faster, stronger. Retiring safe in the knowledge that I had emptied the tank I think would have been easier than this feeling that I gave up. It is heart-breaking.

Not a single day goes by when I don't think about my decision to retire; or more precisely not a day goes by when I don't regret the decision I made to retire. How on earth do I manage this? How do I finally unload the heavy emotional weight that I have been carrying around since 2010, which was compounded by retirement in 2011, and which became even heavier in August 2014 when the Red Roses lifted the trophy?

I have since become self-employed, basing my whole

career on my rugby-playing foundations. Every day therefore I am forced to think about not winning a World Cup. Like a food addict is forced to eat food every day in order to live, I encounter my rugby demons every day in order to make a living. Am I punishing myself in some way? Would it have been easier to walk away and find a 9–5 office job completely unrelated to rugby or sport? I crave that regularly. But no – somehow I have to make my rugby career right. There has to be some sense to it. It has to be a stepping stone to something higher – this can't just be it.

At the time of writing I am still finding it hard to allow myself that time to grieve that I spoke of at the beginning of this book. I never have and I am not sure that I ever will, but time itself is a healer of sorts and importantly I am now recognising that it is OK to start letting go of the pain, to feel all right, not to care so much that we lost by the closest of margins in 2010. That even though I did not become a World Cup-winning captain, life goes on, and in the great grand scheme of things it doesn't matter; it really doesn't. I have to believe this. I have to accept this.

In 2017 I was asked to play in the very first Barbarians' women's team. This is something close to my heart, not just as a rugby fan but as someone who tried to set up this very project about five years ago – there were just too many barriers at that time and as with many things, I was just a few years ahead of my time, planting the seed for others to reap the rewards of the harvest. So when the phone call came, I immediately thought I wanted to do this! Because that is what Catherine Spencer *should* say. Isn't it? But then someone very close spoke to me and helped me realise that there is more to life than rugby. And actually, I don't have to continue to make selfish decisions based around rugby. Mr Right (or Jeremy, to give him his official name) and I were due to get married a few weeks after the Barbarians game. Every time I have played rugby in recent years it has taken me weeks to recover and my knee particularly struggles to recover. I didn't want to hobble down the aisle. My wedding being more important than playing for the Barbarians is OK. And more than that, it is OK to let go of this. It is incredibly difficult and a challenge and if I am honest there is still a part of me that wishes I had said yes to playing in that game, but I know I did the right thing. I have to move on.

The harsh reality is that so often I look back and think that perhaps life would have been better if I had never played rugby for England. The very fact that I think this makes me feel physically sick. How can I really think like this? But I do. Perhaps I would have a great job and be on a fantastic career path by now, using the brain that I have and used to get my 2:1 degree in Philosophy and Sociology. In the run-up to my wedding in 2017 I couldn't help wondering whether I might have got married earlier and had kids by now, rather than worrying about one day being an old mum, or how I may now be too old to have children, after finally meeting the man that I am meant to be with and who, finally, I knew that I wanted to marry. Yet in 2017 I had an engagement ring on my finger, something that I was beginning to think would never happen. At thirty-eight, instead of gearing up for the Barbarians match, I was looking forward to our wedding and trying on dresses and booking venues and tasting food and thinking about decorations and wedding-guest lists.

Throughout my rugby career I was always looking at the next step and it was an easy thing to manage emotionally. It made perfect sense to look up and see where I wanted to head to. It also justified a selfish life. It justified a decision to not work hard at a career beyond rugby. When I retired I didn't know where I was heading. My goalposts disappeared, along with the obvious path in front of me. Like Dorothy losing her yellow brick road in *The Wizard of Oz*, like a 100-metre runner not seeing a straight track ahead of them. Where was I to go? What was I to do? I was near the top of my mountain and I thought I had to descend all the way to the bottom before finding the next one to climb, wasting all of my previous effort and emotion. At the time, I was determined not to crash to the bottom. It was much easier to see where to go next from the top of the mountain range. I did not have to make any descent. I had worked hard to get near the top, so I was damn well going to stay there. I was going to cling on as hard as possible against the powers of gravity trying to drag me back down. In retrospect, and with the benefit of time to reflect, I truly think it would actually have been wise to have descended, to have looked around, looked forward and looked up somewhere else. That would have been OK, and I would not have damaged myself so much with the effort of trying to cling on, of trying to stay near the top.

In 2014 I left a secure paid job plus benefits with the RFU to go to nothing. No guaranteed pay, no pension, no car, no sick pay, no holiday pay. Zilch. But I had an idea and a need and desire to do something different, something better, as well as my own house whose mortgage and associated bills had to be paid. Emotionally and financially it was awful, but I had to get through it. I could not fail; and really I am only just starting to succeed. Despite my positivity and outward confirmation that everything was OK, it was not. It really, really wasn't. It is starting to be now though; in fact it is more than OK. The future looks good and I have started to conquer the challenge of retirement. Started to – nearly a decade later.

In 2018 my life was beginning to set its own goals again; Inspiring Women was going well and I was becoming more businesslike, with some walk to go with the talk. I completed a Human Resource Management level 5 qualification (how I found the time to complete that I don't know), a book was being written and I had wedding photos to sort through. I was starting to look forward more often than looking back. I began to accept that it was all right that this career is taking off as I head towards the big forty rather than fifteen years ago as it would have done for most people. More than seven years after retirement from England, this journey has taken nearly as long as my England career, but it has been tougher. My steps have not been so obvious. As thick cloud fell over the mountain range, I became lost and alone. Sometimes the cloud closes in again and I struggle to see my path. I get lost and I don't know what to think, don't know which way to head, and I lose my self-belief. I want to curl up in a ball, jump under the duvet, close my eyes and go to sleep, shutting the world away. When I was playing rugby, if things were not going my way I knew what to do: I would train harder or analyse a game. I knew exactly where the path led and there was rarely any mountain fog.

Now that I am setting my own goals and trying to lay my own path I question if I am doing the right thing, but I am so far away from any other paths it is too late to turn back. Yet the cloud clears more quickly these days. The fog does not linger. I had to build my confidence as a rugby player and captain and it took a while. Now I am having to build my confidence as a retired rugby player. As Catherine.

The last ever game of rugby that I played was in August 2017 for England Legends v Ireland Legends, held during the 2017 World Cup over in Ireland. The weather was horrific, the game not the best quality, but it was a pleasure to play alongside and against some fantastic names. Listening to Burnsie's chat beforehand was awesome and made me smile a lot! But in that game I damaged my knee again. I had been struggling with it for some time, and looking back now I can see that the problems started when I bent it back in an Aylesford club match against Worcester on a sub-standard all-weather pitch several years previously. I did what I always tended to do – ignored it and hoped that it would get better. I rarely went to the physio at club or country. One season with England I was due to get an award for going a whole season without going to the physio room. Frustratingly, I had to cross the threshold near the end of the season. Gutting! Some players will go to the physio for a broken nail or even more annoyingly because their body hurts. You play rugby, your body will always hurt. Get over it.

Immediately after the 2017 World Cup I went on holiday to Newfoundland with my mum, Jeremy and my aunt. A slightly odd combination it has to be said, but Jeremy got through it and we still got married a few months later!

The whole trip I was struggling to walk. Probably at some point I did need to see someone about it. But I reverted to my old ways, just hoping that it would get better. It did gradually but then I would push it a bit too much in the gym or out for a run and it would get bad again. On Christmas Day 2017 I went out with my two brothers for our traditional Christmas run and my knee felt worse than it ever had. I had to limp back home, still trying to run. A few days later I was getting married. I did not limp down the aisle but I knew that my knee was not right. Finally, I accepted that I really did need to go and see someone. I assumed that my knee would be cleaned out and I could get back to training. I fancied having a crack at a third marathon, really training and trying to post a decent time. I also wanted to compete in the British Indoor Rowing Championships again, this time with some actual training, and see how well I could do. I got into the top ten at my last attempt with a dodgy knee and zero training so my chances had to be good. There were simmering thoughts in the back of my mind that maybe I could even play a bit of rugby again, try and get fit and see if I could make the next Barbarians game, and closer to home I just wanted to be able to go out for a thirty-minute jog. I am lucky enough to live near the sea so jogging is actually a pleasure.

I finally went to see my doctor, who referred me to a specialist knee consultant, and the service I received from the NHS was fantastic. We are so lucky to be able to access good-quality care whoever we are. After an MRI scan I was called back to the consultant. He told me that the good news was that I would not need surgery – but the bad news was that this was because my knee was too far gone. There would be no point in surgery. He explained to me that I had severe cartilage damage and arthritis. He told me very plainly never to run again and that the next step would be a full knee replacement, but they would not want to offer that at this stage in my life. I went back out to my car and I cried. So much. Then I went around to my mum's and cried on her shoulder.

I will never run again. If I am lucky enough to have kids I won't be able to run around with them or run in the parents' race at sports day. And I will never, ever don a pair of rugby boots again. I will never run that third marathon and get the half-decent time that the competitive side of me wanted to accomplish. I will never be able to see just how fast I could go at the British Indoor Rowing Championships. I will never be able to put a pair of trainers on and pop out the front door on the spur of the moment and go for a jog along the seafront. Is it all worth it? I don't know. I'm supposed to say that, yes, it is, aren't I? But do I really think that? My mum had arthritis when she was young, so it is possible that I had a genetic predisposition, but the wear and tear over the long period of my rugby career, plus moments like the Worcester game when I bent my knee back, will all have contributed too.

The consultant told me to swim and cycle. I can't swim at all well and am afraid of putting my head in the water. If someone told me to jump off the side of a pool I would really, really struggle. I am also rubbish at it when I do, on rare occasions, find myself in the water. I did go to swimming lessons for a short while when I was training at Bath University, mainly for them to work out why I would more often than not go backwards when I was trying to go forwards. They could not work it out. A shoulder injury gave me the get-out and I didn't go back. I don't own a bike. I don't understand gears. The two sports I hate the most (apart from football; and I don't count angling or horse-racing because neither, in my opinion, are sports) are swimming and cycling. I will have to one day give myself a mighty swimming challenge to take on, otherwise I won't get in the water. I will need something to aim for and think, yes, I can do that.

Whilst my arthritis diagnosis has been hard it has helped with one thing. I know for certain that I will never play rugby again. I have had to let go of that. This is a decision that has been made for me and I can tell you it is easier to manage and accept than my own decision that I made in 2011. It's just possible that this book is the neat packaging up of my rugby career that I so badly needed. After this hits the shelves, maybe this is it for me. Perhaps it is finally time for me to say goodbye to rugby?

Chapter Thirteen

The Road of the Roses

Since I started playing rugby in the late 1980s the development of women's rugby has been phenomenal. It has come a long way and I am sure will continue to develop, but the road of the Roses over the last decade has been somewhat rocky. This decade of change was propelled significantly by the 2010 Women's Rugby World Cup, especially here in England. Our oh-so-close performance shot us into the media limelight for just enough time to keep the flame burning for a few more years. To not go away entirely. To keep biting at the ankles of editors, broadcasters and, closer to home, the RFU itself. In 2011 the RFUW became fully integrated into the much larger RFU.

The RFUW had already lofted itself from its Portakabin offices in the North Car Park of Twickenham into the main South Stand offices, but in 2011 it became official. Jobs were looked at, departments restructured. The performance staff fell under Rob Andrew's department and the development team (of which I was part at the time) were now integrated into respective geographical areas. My job, along with the other Women's Regional Development Managers, was effectively downgraded from a regional manager to a rugby development officer. Dreams of finally receiving a pay rise were quickly dampened. Despite the shift in role, similar challenges remained, and the success of the development of the game was still reliant on effective relationship-building within the RFU, with our colleagues, with county volunteers and of course with the clubs. On a more positive note, John Steele had been appointed as the new CEO and he was great; there was a really good feeling amongst development staff and those of us working on the shop floor as it were. But the rugby gods were against us again. John was asked to leave the RFU. For fear of being sued for libel, I won't go into any detail. I was devastated. UK Sport, the Youth Sport Trust, the English Institute of Sport and Loughborough University have all since benefitted from his forced departure though.

John came out of that period of time with his personal and professional integrity intact. The RFU, on the other hand, were struggling. Martyn Thomas, then chairman, took over as acting CEO and what followed was a pretty disastrous time for the RFU. The Blackett Report that investigated this was damning and called for the majority of the board to stand down. Men's rugby performances on the pitch were suffering; Martin Johnson, as team manager, was not able to replicate the tremendous leadership of his playing days; players were driven to jumping off ferries in New Zealand and hitting the nightclubs of Queensland mid-tournament. It was a difficult time, and with a home World Cup to host in 2015 worries were snowballing; the media and mainstream press were having a field day. Johnson stepped down in November 2011, but the men's leadership structure and decision-making protocols and processes were still marred with confusion and controversy. Meanwhile the women, after the 2010 final, won the 2011 Six Nations with an emphatic Grand Slam victory, but our on-field pitch achievements were not quite so interesting for the nation's press as the exploits of the men's rugby world, and our column inches were dramatically smaller.

Stuart Lancaster took over as head coach from Johnson and his leadership qualities were immediately placed on a high pedestal by the RFU – with associated pressure building on him I am sure. Lancaster resigned after the 2015 World Cup, taking full responsibility for the men's dismal performance. I had saved up some money to buy two tickets to the England v Wales match in the 2015 World Cup. One for myself and one for Gregory, a gift to say thank you for all his support over the years (and just because he is my twin brother – it's a twin thing!). It cost me a lot of money and I could not really afford it at the time but hey, it was a home World Cup. It was the only time I have ever felt like asking for my money back following a rugby match. The atmosphere before the game was disappointing, the seats were not, in my opinion, good enough considering the amount I spent on them and the game itself was shockingly awful. England crashed out of the World Cup, failing to make it through the pool games, and the leadership qualities of Stuart Lancaster that the RFU had lofted to such dizzy heights after his initial appointment were nowhere to be seen. The hottest ticket in town (well, in the town known as London-By-The-Sea) was the Japan v South Africa game down in Brighton. Every rugby fan, unless of the Springbok variety, was miserable that they were not there on that day to witness the Japanese bring down the South Africans in an incredible victory.

Back to the women: in 2012, the first Six Nations tournament after my retirement, the Red Roses won yet another championship – a Grand Slam in emphatic style, conceding not a single try in the tournament. In 2013 they dropped to third in the Six Nations, and that year focus on the Sevens started to ramp up. This meant that a lot of players were on Sevens contracts and so not available for fifteen-a-side rugby. The Sevens World Cup took place in June that year, and England effectively came sixth, having been knocked out by New Zealand in the Cup quarter-final stage and losing to Australia in the Plate final. Following this, thoughts returned to the fifteen-a-side game with the 2014 World Cup fast approaching, and Sevens players were integrated back into the fifteen-a-side set-up. England, with their full complement of players, picked things up but lost to France in France, which gave them a second-place championship finish.

Confidence leading up to the World Cup was not high, and conversations I had with players confirmed this. A disruptive couple of years due to the swinging pendulum of focus was not helpful. Unlike in 2010, the players did not think that they would win. But thank you, Ireland; New Zealand were knocked out after an incredible defeat by Ireland, and a draw between England and Canada in the pool games (in a game that England really should have won) meant that it was mathematically impossible for the Black Ferns to progress out of their pool due to the cruel twelve-team tournament format; England took their opportunity. The gleam of the trophy that year was hiding the cracks that were starting to appear. But for me, the alarm bells were blaring.

Some people would describe me as 'old school'. I don't mind that, but I would also describe myself as inclusive. Some people would say I am against change; I would say I am loyal to what I believe in. Fifteen minus eight is seven. When you take the inclusiveness out of fifteen-a-side rugby – the game for all shapes and sizes – you get Sevens, the sport that has hooked so many and sucked dry resources, has been destructive in many ways and has destroyed what could have been shining careers for so many. My anti-Sevens stance is not a new thing. Back when it was announced that rugby – sorry, I mean Sevens – was going to be in the Rio Olympics in 2016 my heart sank. Gut instinct is a powerful thing and often right.

My initial concerns surrounded the developing world. I had been out in Uganda several times with the Tag Rugby Trust and had witnessed several men's and women's Elgon Cup matches between Uganda and Kenya. The cup is named after the volcanic mountain that straddles the border. Kenya had been dominating the men's cup for years, with Uganda struggling to compete – but then something changed. Kenya started to chase the Sevens Olympic dream. Resources, attention, interest and kudos all went to the shorter version of the game. The effect on their fifteen-a-side performance was not unsurprising and Uganda pounced, winning the Elgon Cup in 2012 following five years of dominance by Kenya. Since then the cup has changed hands several times.

In the global women's game, the International Rugby Board (now World Rugby) were encouraging developing

nations to focus on Sevens. Why not? It required fewer
people and resources and was a simpler game. But that is
not what people wanted. Women of different shapes and
sizes from all different backgrounds wanted to play rugby.
They wanted to scrum and ruck and maul and do something
different. Sevens was not the answer. What we had been
fighting for over a number of years, what those in Uganda
had been painstakingly developing for years, was in danger
of collapsing because of rugby's own greed. A friend of
mine, Helen Koyokoyo Buteme, has been working tirelessly
for years trying to develop the women's game in Uganda
and has had a lot of success. There have been challenges,
however, as you might imagine, and the emergence of
Sevens has been one of them. Helen said to me:

I love both Sevens and Fifteens but sometimes I wish
that Sevens did not exist because the over-emphasis on
Sevens for women means that women's Fifteens has been
pushed aside in many countries. It is very demotivating
for many Ugandan players because they are not cut out
for Sevens – few players can comfortably play both
codes, meaning that players who only play Fifteens do
not get the chance to represent their country.

Helen has recently been involved with a World Rugby
women's rugby-coaching conference, selected as one of the
world leaders and influencers. I hope that she is listened to.

To be brutally honest, my concerns about Sevens have
only grown. I accept that there is a place for it . . . if I have
to. But I don't want to see the sport that I love destroyed.
I don't want to see a situation where we are competing

with ourselves for participants and I especially don't want to continue to see quantity over quality. And at the elite end, why are we continuing to plough resources and some of our best players into a sport that we are not getting the returns from? I don't see the sense. Anywhere. The period between the 2014 and the 2017 World Cups was rocky to say the least, and post-2017 those rocks became mountains. 'Contractgate' became a thing.

Contractgate emerged after the 2017 World Cup when the short-term contracts that the Women's World Cup squad were on leading up to and during the tournament came to an end. Only Sevens players would continue to receive contracts and any form of paid salary. The reason for this, we were told by the RFU, was that 'women's rugby is cyclical'. Women's rugby is not cyclical – the powers-that-be at our national governing body simply decided that it was for several years leading up to 2014 and beyond 2017, until sense finally seemed to be reached and full-time permanent contracts commenced for twenty-eight fifteen-a-side players in January 2019.

The thing I found hard to chew was, regardless of money and Contractgate, why should our bread and butter, our fifteen-a-side rugby, which is a game for all shapes and sizes, be relegated from any significant level of investment and profile in favour of the shorter form of the game which is suitable only for some members of the athletic physical community because they *might* get a few minutes of fame at the Olympics where, I might add, they are competing for the limelight against a huge number of other sports as well as the standard opposition for profile and investment . . . and breathe! Let me put this rant into context.

After the 2014 World Cup, the emotionally tough one when England Women won, there was a wave of increased interest and a raised profile for the women's game, and rightly so. The squad were awarded Team of the Year at the Sports Personality of the Year Awards, there were stories in all of the papers, receptions were held at Downing Street, bus tours were taking place up and down the country. They didn't all get awarded MBEs like their male counterparts did in 2003, but one step at a time. English women's fifteen-a-side rugby was on a high – and then came a spectacular crash. The game plummeted to a new low in the country. Years of hard work were seemingly undone in just a few days.

This downward trajectory first came to my attention when I was in Italy, attempting to enjoy a romantic weekend away which failed due to my then complete inability to make a good choice when it comes to men, and instead I spent three awful days with one of the most arrogant, selfish men I have ever met. Anyway, as a slight distraction from this I received a phone call from Sky Sports News asking me if I could do a phone interview about Gary Street. Of course I could, but why the sudden interest in Gary? I was confused, until it was explained to me that Gary Street was no longer England head coach; in fact, he was no longer any kind of England coach and did I know anything about this? I carried out the interview knowing nothing but speaking honestly about Gary, talking about him as the good coach and good person that he was. What happened next was more surprising. Graham Smith was staying on to coach the Six Nations but not stepping up to be head coach. Why on earth not? Because Nicky Ponsford was appointed to take over as acting head coach for the 2015 Six Nations, after which Graham Smith would also no longer have a job with the RFU. What was going on?

Nicky, the head of performance at RFU, had played for England a few decades earlier and coached Wasps Ladies in the premiership at not quite the level or standard it is today. What a choice. This, combined with the drain of a significant number of players to the shortened form of the game (twelve of their World Cup winners to be precise) in the build-up to the eagerly anticipated Rio Olympics, meant that England, World Champions, achieved their worst ever result in the Six Nations, finishing in a pitiful fourth place. They only managed to record victories against Scotland and Italy and failed to score a single point against Wales. Well done. Success in the Six Nations could and should have been a great marketing platform for the women's game, a springboard to some significant sponsorship perhaps? More column inches, more screen time? But no. For the first time ever I was, quite frankly, embarrassed to be associated with the game.

Roll on three years, England Women lost the 2017 World Cup to a New Zealand team which completely outclassed the Red Roses, who were overcome by the power of their forward pack. The Roses' confidence and strength were bullied to smithereens by the Black Ferns, who were reminiscent of the England pack of days gone by, coached by Graham Smith. And the Olypmic Sevens? They finished without a medal, with minimal press coverage and zero club pathway to stack it up.

What has really been the outcome for England following

Rio, where Team GB – sorry, England plus one Welsh player – managed to come fourth after huge investments in time and money? The men got a silver medal but were outclassed and out-supported by Fiji, the global nations' favourite when it comes to seven-a-side rugby. Even I, an ardent un-supporter of Sevens, used to run around the garden with my twin brother, throwing the ball to each other through our legs chanting 'Fiji style, Fiji style'. But has there been an influx of players rocking up at rugby clubs up and down the country because they may have glimpsed a few minutes of Sevens on the TV in the middle of the night? I don't think so. And even if this were the case, it is not Sevens that would be waiting for them but a game that would be unrecognisable from their Olympic screens. Proper rugby.

Why are we pushing Sevens so much? Because it is less muddy? More feminine? It was seen for a while as the saviour of women's rugby, the thing that would finally propel the game into some sustainable limelight. Wrong. But I think there is finally a shift back to focus on our core game. Our mauls are safe, I think. The Sevens thing, whilst I am sure it will not go away, no longer resides alone at the top of the pecking order. As mentioned, in 2018 it was announced that permanent contracts would be awarded to our top twenty-eight fifteen-a-side players, along with New Zealand and France, who offer their fifteen-a-side players part-time contracts; the longer form of the game is seeing some real positive development.

Our club game also seems to be strengthening at elite level, though there are still the continuing challenges for the majority of clubs to secure enough players to fulfil fixtures.

The RFU has proudly announced huge participation numbers in the women's game but I would say that we need to question the validity of those statistics. They may well refer to registered players but they are not players turning up week in, week out. The figures, as in the men's game, hide a participation problem that the RFU don't seem to want to recognise. As Vic Reeves famously once said, '88.2 per cent of all statistics are made up on the spot.'

Whilst gains are being made in the women's game strides still need to be made. We are still seen as second-class citizens when it comes to our sport, but things can change. It just needs some dynamic, forward-thinking, brave leaders at the top of our game. I wonder if we will ever get them.

In September 2018 I wrote the following article for the Rugby Paper:

At the early stages of this year's Tyrrells Women's Premiership, as we start to build towards autumn internationals, I ask, where are the fans? Will they turn up? Harlequins, Saracens and Wasps are emerging as front runners already on the pitch with Bristol and Loughborough also showing promise but what of the off-field development?

Many empty seats at stadiums paints a less than positive picture. That is what really counts

Last year Harlequins Ladies played a stand-alone match at the Twickenham Stoop against Richmond and attracted a crowd of nearly 5,000. This is an impressive figure. To put this in some context, whilst Bristol Bears men attracted over 25,000 to their opening fixture two weeks ago against Bath, Worcester did not quite make the 8,000 mark and Newcastle just scraped past 7,000. In the men's championship focus has been directed towards Ealing Trailfinders who are struggling to attract more than 1,000 supporters to their games. But it was only down to Harlequins' heavy promotion of their game that the crowds came. Normal Tyrrells Premier 15's spectator numbers last season were much lower. Much lower. But Harlequins have proved that the spectators are there if we provide them with information and the crowds will become fans if they feel like there is something worth cheering. Fans are regular supporters, fully engaged and feeling as if they are part of the team. It takes two seconds to post a supporting hashtag on social media, as is so often done, but our physical presence speaks louder. We need to vote with our feet as it were and #Showup. We have to demonstrate that we have a product of value in order to build a fan base.

England Women kick off their Quilter autumn international season with a cracker of a fixture against America at Allianz Park. America came fourth in last year's World Cup and are my international team to watch for this season. If they can replicate part of their World Cup form we will be in for a treat. We need to build this game up, we need to promote it, we need to market it and we need to place it on the pedestal worthy of its level. It is possible to fill Allianz Park. Why not? But it won't magically happen, it will take work.

England then face Canada at Castle Park stadium, Doncaster. I am all for taking the game around the country, I think it is positive (the men are following suit in 2019, trekking north up the M1 to Newcastle) but the stadium has a capacity of just 5,000. Please aim higher. How to devalue a women's international in one easy step. If we think that we are going to fail, if we don't have confidence that we can achieve, if we don't set our sights high, how can we expect our players to do any better on the pitch? Ten years ago, playing at a 5,000-capacity stadium would have been a step up for our international team. Now, in 2018, surely it is a step back.

Ireland comes last at Twickenham and I have no doubt that 90 per cent of the crowd in attendance for the men's game will have no idea that the women's game is following. So we need to clearly market these games but we also need to promote their value. Women's rugby may seem like a joke to some but it doesn't always need to be that way. Remember the joke of the car world? Skoda. How did it transform from a car with a stigma to a car with some class? I remember getting a lift home from school with a friend in a Skoda. I sank down in the back seat so that no one would see me and associate me with the car, and I even reconsidered my friendship after the dramatic realisation that their mum drove a Skoda! This is women's rugby. People are still scared to associate themselves with the sport.

More recently a women's rugby coach that I work with requested some kit that did not mention the word 'women's' because he was fed up of not being taken seriously. Women's rugby still suffers the Skoda stigma. But things can and do change. It is now OK to want a Skoda, to own a Skoda, to be seen driving a Skoda. In 1991, Skoda sold just approximately 191,000 cars.

The car was the number one laughing stock of the car world; 'Why does a Skoda have a heated windscreen? To keep your hands warm when you push it.' 'How do you double the price of a Skoda? Fill up the tank.' 'What do you call a Skoda with a sunroof? A skip'. The list of classic jokes goes on! But something incredible happened and in 2010 they sold more than 750,000 cars and in 2017 this figure was nearing a million. How? The credible, widely respected, successful car company VW bought and invested heavily in Skoda and with effective, targeted branding and marketing the joke has turned into something quite different. Who is laughing now?

The Tyrrells Premiership clubs are trying; Wasps Ladies played their home fixture at Ealing Trailfinders this weekend rather than their normal Acton ground. It will be interesting to watch this development and building relationship. Perhaps it will help to boost both parties.

A number of women's clubs, including Wasps, do not have headline sponsors as we commence the second full season of the premiership, and whilst Tyrells have come on board as the league sponsor I would argue that they are not VW enough. A higher level of investment is required; an innovative, slightly disruptive, ambitious, forward-thinking strategy is required across the game from club level to our elite Red Roses. We need influencers and experts to come together to turn what is sometimes treated as the joke of rugby into something successful. Land Rover, I know that you love rugby, but Skoda, do you fancy bringing your expertise to women's rugby?

*

Harlequins are aiming to reach 8,000 for their next crowd milestone figure and I am sure that by the time this book hits the shelves they will have achieved that. I don't think that Allianz Park will have been filled for the 2018 autumn internationals but one day it could be. We can't be happy with just OK; we need to aim higher. We need to look around, look up and look forward.

And I want to refer to Will Carling's famous line in 1995 describing the RFU's council members as 'fifty-seven old farts'. He had a point. I love the fact that the game is run by volunteers and depends on volunteers despite the size of the RFU workforce – that's what makes our game great. But let the women out of the kitchen and into the committee room. That is where we should be focusing our efforts: men and women joining forces to continue ensuring that this great contact game of ours remains great. The sport is still overwhelmingly male on and off the pitch and deep down I am not sure if this will ever really see any significant change. I am sure that women will still be playing their club games on Sunday afternoons up and down the country at dead times. The first-team pitches will always be, for the most part, reserved for the men regardless of what level their senior women's team are playing at. But the game is changing and perhaps clubs will start to see the increase in women's teams as their saviour. Men's teams are in decline, whatever figures the RFU choose to share with us. Clubs that once put out four senior men's teams, a colts team and a vets team on a Saturday afternoon now struggle to put out two, with some struggling to even fulfil their first-team fixtures. And that isn't really the fault of the clubs. Societal pressures are different now from what they once were and the desire for flexible, pay-as-you-go sport is increasing; so too is the world of 'CrossFit' and the like. I don't mind that rugby is a minority sport – I would never want it to become like football because it would lose its heart and its values – but what I do want is for rugby to be an accessible sport for those who do chose to participate, regardless of gender, background or sexuality.

Back to the road of our Roses. Whilst I have vocally supported the move to ensure professional contracts for fifteen-a-side players, it is bittersweet for me. I supported it because of my passionate belief in equality. In this case not just gender equality but equality between the Sevens and Fifteens to allow our players a fair choice. I am extremely pleased that the likes of Emily Scarratt, Mo Hunt and Jess Breach have returned to the longer form of the game. But equality was my only reason to support the move and does not reflect what I truly think, and that is that I miss the old days of proper rugby. I grew up as a rugby fan. I used to love seeing the names of rugby players on the screen along with their professions: police officer, farmer, teacher, surgeon, solicitor. It meant more to me. Real people with substance. As the men's game went professional in 1995 this of course started to disappear. But this substance, this realness, continued in the women's game. I feel proud that I played for England at a high level on top of working. It has added meaning. It is inspiring. When I hear current male players talk about their rugby careers at events I am sorry to say that I switch off. It bores me. We put them up on a pedestal, we think they are heroes for getting paid to do what for the majority of us is a hobby. Well done for getting up in the morning, going to the gym (most of us have to pay for this luxury), going to the club to hang out with team mates (a luxury for many of us in our spare time at weekends), watching some rugby on television (many of us have to pay heavy monthly subscriptions to view any rugby) and then going home and playing a computer game or two. And while I accept that they occupy these pedestals because they have worked hard in the gym or on the pitch – though on some match days this is hard to imagine – I can't see any of myself in them.

The same will happen to our female 'stars'. At some point in the not-too-distant future our elite players will also start to be paid by clubs, as well as country, and their lives will start to mirror those of their male counterparts. And the fan in me is no longer alive. I am no longer a rugby fan because of this move to professionalism and it makes me sad. I am a fan of the sport, I enjoy watching a maul or a good tackle or a well-executed line-out, but I also feel disappointment when I see over-trained, overpaid athletes who spend more time in the gym than they do understanding the true essence of the game. I laughed when I watched Italy confuse England in the men's Six Nations several years ago. They used the complex rules to their advantage and got themselves in the way of England around the tackle area. England automatically assumed that they were cheating. It was much easier to blame them than to work out a solution for themselves. The best part was when we watched James Haskell and Dylan Hartley trying to ask the referee what was going on. He explained to them very simply that he was not their coach. Classic! Very quickly after I saw what Italy were doing, my immediate response was that England needed to start picking the ball through the middle of the ruck, which would force the loose Italian defenders to commit to the breakdown area and thus create the needed space for the England scrum-half to release the ball to his backs. These paid professionals on the pitch could not work this out for themselves through the whole of the first half. It took someone to tell them at half-time what to do. How worrying. We are not creating rugby players at the top level of the English game. It seems to me that the rugby is being taken out of them and it is sad to watch. I still watch matches, in the hope that I will see some spark of personality or intuition. I hope that the women do not follow this route. We don't have to do everything the men do. We can learn from their mistakes.

The road of the Roses will always be bumpy; the minority within a minority sport will always have to battle. In the past those battles have hardened the players. The significant away victory over France in 2006 was only possible because of the fight of the players, particularly in the forwards. Battle-hardened, tough but passionate. We had to fight to be on that pitch so we were going to do everything possible to make sure we relished the opportunity. Graham Smith created the best pack in the world for many years. He was blessed with natural talent but he also delved into our personalities. He knew what made us tick, he understood what we have had to fight for and he utilised that power. That power does not exist any more; the battles are changing in their nature and our elite players, our Red Roses, are now able to go about their rugby business without having to fight for it. And whilst we may be seeing longer passes, faster running, more complicated moves, I fear that, especially in the forwards, we are losing a tough breed of player. I don't think we will ever see the forward packs again that we saw in Graham Smith's day. For me, the 2017 World Cup final started to demonstrate this. Our coaches now need to find another way to toughen up their players because it won't come from their battles to be on the pitch nor, from January 2019, will it come from their understanding of juggling precious time in order to become the best player they could possibly be. Sometimes things can become too easy mentally and that will start to have an effect on the pitch.

Just before the 2018 autumn internationals it was announced by England Rugby that Courtney Lawes, second row, would not be playing because he had slept in the wrong kind of bed. Seriously? Where are our tough rugby players? The second row is the engine room – what is happening? I would love to have seen the reaction of Martin Johnson when he read that news. If it was anything like mine, he would have been thinking what an embarrassment it was to our sport. Too much cotton wool, not enough grit. Please, please, please do not introduce too much cotton wool into the women's game.

Chapter Fourteen
The Power of Rugby

A few years ago, I was in a bar talking to a 25-year-old, listening to them tell me about their international rugby. Not so unusual an occurrence. I watched them become incredibly animated and I could see the passion and love in their eyes for the game that had changed their life. The 25-year-old was a woman and the bar was in a town called Jinja in Uganda. Christine plays rugby for the Lady Cranes – Uganda's national women's rugby team. Christine told me that not only did rugby give her the courage to do something different but it gave her the reason. Being female, twenty-five, unmarried and with no children was not the norm in Uganda, but through sport and particularly through rugby Christine and her team mates were demonstrating that other choices exist. Until that moment I knew that sport was good for us mentally as well as physically but I didn't truly understand the full extent of its power. Before I continue, however, I should explain why and how I was in that bar in Jinja, Uganda.

In 2006, a couple of weeks before heading off with the squad to Canada for the World Cup, I was invited to a South

West awards evening with Katy Storie and Kim Oliver. I listened to a presentation about a trip to India where a group of volunteers had taught tag rugby to children. I sat there thinking that I love rugby, I love travelling and that I had to get involved! But shortly after this, off we went to Canada to compete in the World Cup and this idea was pushed to the back of my mind, but serendipity is my favourite word for a reason. After 2006 Sophie Hemming and I started to train with an incredible coach called Geoff Moon at Bristol rugby (A top man who very sadly died in 2019; he will be missed by so many.). He was there working with their academy but also delivered to me and Sophie on a weekly basis. He didn't have to, he was not getting paid to and took personal time out to do so, but like so many coaches in rugby he went above and beyond to support the development of the game and its players. We did loads of really good core work (front-row focused in a way) but really useful for me. The things I could do on a Swiss Ball back then amaze me, now I can barely sit on one without wobbling! At one of these sessions we were being shadowed by a younger girl who had aspirations to play rugby at a higher level. She was being chaperoned by a rugby coach and general rugby legend called Gary Townsend. It just so happened that at the time he was involved with tag rugby and as a result the Tag Rugby Trust. He had provided the first bag of tag kit to take to Uganda in 2002. We got talking at that session in Bristol and as a consequence he introduced me to the trustees of TRT. And there started one of the best, most fulfilling and valuable rugby relationships of my life.

I met with Rob Newman, one of the trustees, who lived in

Portishead. I had just been awarded the England captaincy so when I met Rob he presented me with a pub lunch, a cup of tea and a proposal for me to become an ambassador for the trust. They wanted me to be involved? Just a girl from Folkestone? Really? It was the first time I had been asked to be any kind of ambassador and I felt honoured. I felt a bit of a fraud but I was so keen to be involved with TRT that I accepted. I took the role on with the understanding on both sides that my time may be a little limited as I was working full-time to earn money as an office manager and then the rest of my time was taken up working as England captain. But having learned about the trust I was so eager to find the time to travel out and see their impact first hand. It was also important to me that I travelled whilst I was England captain. I did not want to wait until I had retired. I spoke to the England coaches and they allowed me to miss one summer training camp, which enabled me to travel to Uganda on a volunteer tour with TRT. This was the only England training I ever missed. Although it was difficult to miss training at this point in my captaincy journey, as explained earlier in this book, it was, in relation to my wider world, completely and utterly worth it.

I joined a volunteer tour to Uganda in 2009 and had one of the most inspiring, humbling and life changing experiences of my life. There were approximately twenty of us who travelled out from the UK, including a wide variety of individuals; some rugby players, some with no experience of the game. The joy of tag rugby is that it is such a simple game that after just a few introductory sessions anyone can coach the game. Tag Rugby Trust started life in 2002 when two founding trustees headed out to a small village in

Uganda with a handful of rugby balls and some tag belts. A man called Grandpa Joe greeted the visitors that time and although neither he nor the other elders in the village nor the kids had ever seen a rugby ball they welcomed these strange people into their community. After some coaching a game of tag rugby took place and thus began the Tag Rugby Development Trust, as it was known then.

The trust has come a long way since then and although tag rugby continues to provide the vehicle for engagement the focus is more on off-pitch personal and community development. From work experience programmes to community volunteering projects, to road-safety education, to drama productions, from mixed-ability engagement to mentoring programmes, the work that Tag Rugby Trust, as it is now called, has delivered over the years is quite simply phenomenal. It has had a positive impact upon the lives of hundreds of thousands of young people around the world, and also the lives of people like me. It is just incredible. I am now a patron of the charity and Martin Hansford (chair), Rob Newman, Trevor Martingell and the other trustees inspire me beyond belief. These are the people whose voices should be heard. This is where the real values of rugby are delivered. It is not all about what happens in the confines of Twickenham or on our television screens. These are the true legends of rugby.

I have so many incredible memories of my first away trip with TRT in 2009. We stayed in tents on the side of the rugby pitch in Jinja for our first week, before heading to a town called Mbale for a second week, finishing off with a few days in the capital, Kampala. On the trip we were joined by local volunteers. This is the reason why TRT is so successful. It is not a case of drop in, have your photo taken, get the T-shirt, then head home and forget about it. Far from it. The focus is on sustainable development and the local volunteer community is key. The work of TRT continues every day throughout the year, the volunteer trips from the UK provide some momentum, engagement and of course an injection of some funding to help provide more equipment, but that is the tip of the iceberg in terms of action on the ground. I was to learn a lot about TRT over the years, but it was this trip in 2009 that ignited my passion.

On that first trip, I took no phone, I took no watch, I just took myself, a few pairs of shorts and some T-shirts and a couple of my England playing shirts to present at different times. For the first week we were split into small coaching groups and sent off to different schools in and around Jinja, culminating with a tournament on the Friday morning. We coached as many children as possible throughout the week and then selected ten kids from each school to represent their school at the tournament – five boys and five girls. The first school that I worked at was the Army School. The school provides boarding places for children with a parent in the army, and many of the children had become orphans. The living conditions were very basic but for many of the kids it was their home, 365 days of the year.

Being able to take part in the coaching week was hugely enjoyable, but as the days went by and the kids understood that only ten would be representing the school at the tournament on the Friday, emotions started to run high – for them and for us. Representing the school was a great honour but it also meant a day out of the confines of the school. A rare excursion. The school was great though, and transported lots of the other kids in their army trucks on the day so that they could support their team. This in turn created an incredible atmosphere on tournament day. That season TRT had won the International Rugby Board development award and took the trophy out with them to Uganda and other tour destinations. We took the trophy to the Army School with us one day and showed it to all the children taking part and explained to them that, really, they had won the award. It was their award. They crowded around that trophy with such joy and excitement on their faces, it was hugely emotional.

It was really tough selecting a team of ten from over 200 excited kids but we somehow managed it and also selected our captain. He was called Joel and was one of the smallest players at the tournament. He was a fantastic player and also had the biggest smile on his face that I have ever seen. As one of the team coaches I could not believe how competitive I was feeling. We got to the final of the whole tournament but lost in the final. If I had not been coaching perhaps they would have won – I am jinxed when it comes to finals! In Jinja that week our group coached at three schools and it was really hard work. This trip was definitely not a holiday. We would get a lift to the Army School first thing, then would get ourselves to the other schools and back home again, either walking or on bicycle taxis known as *boda bodas*. The *boda bodas* were hilarious. At the beginning of the week the taxi cyclists would crowd around us – all wanting business from the *mazungo* or white people – but by the end of the week they were not so keen. Why? Because we were generally bigger and heavier than them

– especially Adam in our group who was about 6'5"! We were always laden down with rugby kit, making us even heavier, and with only the power of their legs transporting themselves and us and kit on not the easiest of road surfaces, it made it very hard work.

At the end of the week we waved goodbye to Jinja and headed up to a different town, Mbale, to deliver the second week's programme. One of the things that made this second week so incredible was a parade through the town of all the kids taking part in the Friday tournament. I will never, ever forget it. The parade was accompanied by a brass band and the kids all waved their school flags with absolute pride. The roads were shut, and carrying a very large inflatable rugby ball we caused quite a stir. But a good one. We walked for about two miles, and very early on, one of the supporters in the team I was looking after was struggling with a bad ankle. If one of the kids says anything about being hurt you know that they really are. Generally they never mention anything and just keep going forever. So I carried this girl on my back for most of the way. She was one of the older kids and let's just say that it was good training!

Talking of training, my personal training continued whilst I was in Uganda. I took out a specially prepared programme of mainly body-weight strength exercises along with the usual speed, endurance, shuttles and so on. I have memories of forcing myself out of my tent in the first week while it was still dark to complete my training before our coaching day started. It was tough but I was encouraged by a good number of the local volunteers who joined in. Some of them were playing for the women's national team so they were great training partners. In the second week I found a couple of decent-sized blocks of concrete at the bottom of the site where we were camping so I used these for some weight training. Martin, the chairman of TRT, said that one day when I had finished and gone off to get showered, one of the UK volunteers (a young lad about twenty years old) who had seen me lift the concrete blocks decided to walk over and do the same. He could not lift them off the ground! He never said anything to me, but Martin let me know his secret!

The kids that we coached were incredible, but their backgrounds certainly put things into perspective. Some of the poverty that we saw was tough to process. The focus of TRT has changed, and whilst tag rugby coaching for kids is still at the centre, the focus is very much on community development and coaching education along with other areas of skill development. TRT creates CVs for local volunteers through their time volunteering with the trust, which in turn helps them to apply for paid employment. TRT has also, as a by-product, helped to create some national team players whose first experience of playing rugby was through TRT at their school or within their community. The trust 'Builds futures through Rugby' and its existence in many ways perfectly describes the power of rugby.

In 2012 I went to Mexico with three of the trustees – Martin, Rob and Chris Tapper – to deliver a coaching education project. We went to the outskirts of Guadalajara and based our programme in two academy centres developed by the famous Mexican footballer Rafael Márquez. The centres were in challenging areas. Fathers were generally absent from children's lives and more often than not had been killed or were in prison for drugs-related offences. The day-to-day activities of the centres were run by local mothers who were, in return, trained by the charity. The kids in turn were encouraged to attend the centres in the afternoon following school (if they went) and they would not only get fed but could take part in sports along with additional education. We were introducing tag rugby to the programme but we weren't coaching the kids ourselves; we were educating the mothers who would then coach the kids. The women turned up for their coaching education with incredible displays of eyeshadow. I loved it! On the face of it they were the most unlikely of rugby coaches. They spoke no English and my Spanish was minimal, but the simplicity of tag rugby meant that in just a few days they became coaches. They were brilliant. And in learning something new, stepping out of their comfort zone, they also became role models for their own children and their wider communities.

On that same trip I delivered a coaching session to both the men's and women's university rugby teams. I have delivered adult coaching sessions in a number of locations around the world, including the middle of Kolkata, and it is a real privilege to be able to share some of the knowledge that I have picked up along the years. In Mexico, the session unfortunately coincided with some strong winds which picked up sand and grit and blew it through the air. A piece of grit went into my eye; the next day I had to go to hospital to get the grit removed and was consequently then ordered to wear an eyepatch for the rest of the week. Apart from providing entertainment for the kids, who thought it was hilarious, it provided something of a depth perception challenge for me. Catching a rugby ball was not the easy, natural action it usually was. It also reminded me of a session that Giselle Mather delivered during her time as England coach when she made us wear eyepatches. It forced us to look around more, to turn our heads and scan the pitch. It was a valuable lesson for me as someone who tended to get a little tunnel vision on the pitch. That training did not help me in Mexico though!

Another aspect of TRT that has been so valuable is the inclusion of mixed-ability children and adults into their programmes. In Mexico we delivered a session to a number of young adults and children with various forms of Down's syndrome. They were fantastic. Some of them were happy to just run around and chase tags, but towards the end of the session for the most part we were playing full games of tag rugby, no different to any other coaching sessions. In India we delivered to a school for deaf children. For most of the group this was their first introduction to rugby, but within an hour my group were playing a full game of tag rugby. This was a quick progression by anyone's standards. This simple game, the power of it, allowed me to communicate with a group of deaf children from a particularly poor school in India. TRT has always treated mixed-ability groups as they would anyone else. On a recent tour to Uganda we included the special needs school in the main tournament. The opposition teams were great and did not bat an eyelid. We had two children who were in wheelchairs in the team. One of our volunteers would push the wheelchair, and if the child had the ball on their lap at the time the opposition would remove their tag as normal. In one particular game the volunteer pushing one of the chairs was a former GB rugby league player and captain, Lindsay Anfield. She has been on a few trips with TRT, and that year had brought a group of student league players to volunteer. We ended up that tour playing a full test against Uganda women. Claire Purdy also came out on that trip and took her place in the team alongside some of the league players and recently retired Ugandan players. It was hot, the playing surface tough, but I absolutely loved playing that game. An incredible moment.

In the tag tournament where Lyndsey was pushing the wheelchair, the ball was in the child's lap and Lyndsay eyed the game in front of her while pushing the wheelchair. Her competitive nature came to the fore and her pace picked up and up and up until she was sprinting full-tilt, pushing this wheelchair down the grass and sand pitch. Unfortunately, she didn't spot the big divot in front of her (sometimes they just cannot be avoided) and, in slow motion it seemed, because we all knew what was going to happen but could not do anything about it, the wheelchair along with its inhabitant went flying through the air. We all held our breath, anxious of the outcome. We needn't have been so concerned. The chair may have picked up a few bumps but the child had such a huge grin on her face it was, I think, my favourite moment of that trip. It was priceless!

In India we delivered to an incredible school called KISS in Bhubaneswar. KISS, the Kalinga Institute of Social Sciences, is no ordinary school. It provides free, residential education for some of the poorest children in India, with the aim of eradicating poverty and empowering disadvantaged sections of society. Last year they had a remarkable 25,308 students and served an unfathomable

100,000 meals every single day. When I was there in 2011 the number of students was closer to half this number, but still an impressive feat of logistics. It was awe-inspiring just being there. Our tournament was held at KISS with teams from the school along with other schools in the area. Somehow I had agreed, or been volunteered, to wear a big mascot outfit during the day that had been donated to us by London Irish Rugby Club. In India, in incredibly hot conditions, I had to run around in a thick greyhound costume. There were thousands of kids watching around the pitch and so at our mid-tournament break there I was jogging around the pitch, not really being able to see anything, followed by thousands of screaming, happy kids. It was quite an experience. I then had to quickly get changed, rehydrate and get back out on the pitch to referee the anticipated tournament final. The pitch was the biggest tag rugby pitch I have seen; the game was one of the fastest I have ever experienced and was played in front of one of the biggest crowds I have ever witnessed. The final went to extra time and I had to be on top of my game as referee. The game then went on to extra-extra time before one of the teams managed to finally score the winning try. It was an incredible day and one that I will never forget. KISS is still producing a number of good rugby players who have gone on to represent their country.

A couple of years ago I supported Gregory, who is a teacher, in taking a group of his students to Zambia where they took part in coaching local government schools. The power of rugby took a slightly different tack on this tour and a moment that will stay with me a lifetime took place away from any school coaching or rugby pitch. The UK school that Gregory taught at was in a fairly deprived area. The students, and Gregory, fundraised hard for two years in order to pay for the costs of the trip: flights, food, accommodation and so on. Many of the students did not venture beyond their own town boundary in the UK and quite possibly never would, but fourteen of them took on this incredible adventure. They were a brilliant bunch, stepping into a world they had no experience of, and the nerves were obvious at the beginning. The group and individuals within it really blossomed through the trip and the impact of this new experience was obvious. They also really understood the aims of TRT – that these went beyond the rectangle of a rugby pitch.

As a treat at the end of the tour we went down to Victoria Falls. As well as seeing the waterfalls, there was also more wildlife in this area of Zambia. One of Gregory's students had always loved animals and her favourite animals were elephants. One day we saw some elephants. We all knew how much she wanted to see one and when we did Gregory and I turned around in our bus to look at her reaction. She was sitting with tears streaming down her face. It was overwhelming for her, a life dream had come true, all because of the power of tag rugby. She had never, before this trip, set foot on a rugby pitch, had never passed or caught the strange egg-shaped ball, but without the opportunity of this trip, who knows if she would ever have experienced that moment. It was the values of TRT that drew her to Zambia, and the realisation of her dream was a massive bonus for her.

One of the more recent projects I have been involved with is the development of a programme called FITR –

Female Inspiration Through Rugby. FITR, like TRT, uses rugby as the vehicle to engage but its reach goes far beyond. The programme provides positive personal, social and developmental opportunities, activities and support to young women and girls. Our three main areas of focus are to develop female leaders and mentors, to enable and encourage life choices and to support education in school, in sports and in careers. The programme is running in Harare, Zimbabwe, and has now developed to other areas of the country, and we hope to expand to other countries that TRT is working in.

The key to the success of the programme is centred around the mentor programme. Quite simply, by training and developing one mentor we can reach a whole community. Our mentors work with younger girls who are taking part in existing TRT activities or through partner organisations such as the Girls Legacy Trust. Our mentors will not only coach rugby but also provide other opportunities for development and support. The girls they work with are generally growing up in challenging conditions in high-density areas. For example, girls are not always able to access the same schooling opportunities as boys. I met one seventeen-year-old girl on one of my trips out to a rural area called Domboshava in eastern Zimbabwe. At the age of seventeen she had not been to school, ever. Not a single day. When I met her, she was taking part in a tag rugby session with other girls from her community that the FITR mentors were running, and her confidence was already growing.

Two other areas of focus have come about after direct conversations with different female members of challenged communities in Zimbabwe. I spoke to many girls, young leaders and older 'aunties' who offer support as best they can, who said that the girls were scared to use the Internet. They thought that only bad things were on the Internet, rather than seeing it as the educational tool it could be. The second focus area was on the importance of providing a safe space for the girls; somewhere that they can chat to others about their challenges or their hopes and dreams without fear of being overheard by an elder in their own community. For this reason, we built a FITR clubhouse in the grounds of Harare Sports Club and we aim, funding dependent, to go on to provide these safe places in other communities where they are needed. Also in the centre there will be a number of computers, donated by Africa Computers, that can be used to help to educate. The clubhouse will be used for other members of the TRT and rugby community but it will be FITR owned, managed by FITR and there will be times when it will be for exclusive FITR use.

I have now been on nearly twenty trips with TRT, to Uganda, Ghana, Zambia, Kenya, Zimbabwe, Mexico and India, and probably could write a whole book just about the incredible work of the trust and its volunteers here in the UK and abroad. If you want to know more, please get in contact and ask me, because the words I have written in this chapter do not describe the full extent of their positive impact. They do not do TRT justice. They are quite simply incredible.

The power of rugby and more specifically the influence of TRT resulted in my completing two marathons to raise money for the charity. The first time I completed the

26.2 miles was in April 2011 when we took on the Paris Marathon. I had not done any marathon training but I had very recently retired from England duty so my fitness levels were still high. I thought I would be fine. I wore a scruffy old England rugby T-shirt and a pair of really old-school rugby shorts – they had pockets and everything. No expensive running gear for me – I didn't want the 'all the gear, no idea' line aimed at me.

That first time sheer stubbornness got me round the route. It was the hottest day of the year in Paris (or felt like it) and a higher percentage than usual dropped out or simply collapsed on the side of the road. For this reason, I decided to run quite slowly – I did get overtaken by a wine barrel being pushed round, a man running backwards and an old lady who looked about twice the size of me. At that point I was a little confused but I simply accepted that I was not a runner. I trotted around very slowly and came in over five hours. Martin Hansford and his brother Gareth had finished about two hours earlier, and when I met them at the end they looked like they had done no more than run for a bus. That evening we went for *steak frites* (when in Paris . . .), after which they suggested that we trot up to the Sacré-Cœur. At this point it was all I could do to simply to walk to the restaurant toilet, and promptly declined. I could not walk for quite some time but I had a sense of motivation travelling back to England on the train the next day, that I would train and compete again the following year and get a good time. I really would!

The second time I did it, I think two years later, my twin brother Gregory ran with me. This time I had done some training but it had been hampered by a broken toe that I picked up in a club rugby game. By the time the marathon came round, because of my toe injury I had not done any running training for several months, but I was determined to get round again. The first half was good. We made it to the halfway point in not long over two hours, which was a really good time for me. But then my knee failed me. I told Gregory to go on, to save himself and in *Last of the Mohicans* style told him that 'I would find him'; I staggered/limped the second half – probably the least enjoyable day of my life. The second half took me nearly twice as long as the first half. Gregory, in contrast, ran his second half quicker than the first. Typical. I should have known then that my knee was not right. I never ran another marathon and never will, but I like to think that one day I will take on another challenge to raise funds for TRT.

The power of rugby manifests itself in many ways; it feels like an appropriate time to talk in more detail about a good friend of mine – Sophie Hemming. I have mentioned her already but I want to describe just how inspiring she has been to me. Sophie, as I mentioned in Chapter One, missed out on selection to the 2006 World Cup but she was there in 2010 and 2014. I don't think that there were many in 2006 who would have predicted what an impact Sophie would have in an England shirt; in fact there were many people at that point who quite confidently would have stated that Sophie was not good enough to represent her country at all. Sophie was not the most naturally talented rugby player I have met, but what she did have was incredible determination, a work ethic like no other and a devotion to the cause that made mine feel like that of a mere minnow at times. Sophie worked and worked and worked, she got fitter, she did her homework, she became an expert at her trade and became, I am confident to write in print, the best technical scrummager in the world, male or female. There were many onlookers and actually some of Sophie's own team mates (backs mainly) who didn't understand quite how good Sophie was. Her direct opposition knew. Rocky Clark, her long-time England team mate, knew. I knew, her team mate, captain, training partner and friend. I knew.

We lived very close to each other in Bristol and completed the majority of our training sessions together. Sophie often said that she spent more time with me than she did with Tom, her boyfriend whom she lived with at the time (now her husband!), and this was probably true. We were a good influence on each other. Sophie helped me to develop a stronger work ethic; she would make sure that not a single section of every prescribed training session was left uncompleted. It was important to her that everything was ticked off as it should be. In turn I taught Sophie the importance of rest. That was my talent! But in all seriousness, this was really important.

My first strength-and-conditioning coach who supported me when I broke into England A (then simply called England) for the first year advised me that I should always, always mark my rest time in my training schedule planners before anything else. For Sophie this was important; she had to start listening to her body and rest when needed, even if it meant part of her sessions did not get ticked off, because not only was Sophie an England player, she was also a full-time vet, and a large-animal vet at that. She would often be on call through the night, and she might have been called out to a farm at 2 a.m., but she would still, without fail, be at Bath University on time for our early-morning training sessions. When other players, particularly students, complained of not having enough time, I told them that there is no such thing. You will make time if you really want something.

I also understood that Sophie's time was precious. One Friday evening I was delivering a talk to a rugby club for a friend of mine in Birmingham. They kindly put me up in a hotel room for the night, but I got up at 4:30 a.m. to drive back to Bristol to take part in our scheduled pitch-sprint session before Sophie needed to go to work.

The power of rugby turned Sophie into a world-class player, a World Champion with over seventy caps to her name. For me it created a great friendship that will remain forever.

Chapter Fifteen
The Subtle Suffragette

At the beginning of this book I shared my struggles about being described as 'someone who has gone before', a person who laid foundations for others to succeed in achieving my dream of winning a World Cup, whilst all I could do was look on. Since retiring I still often feel bitter, angry and resentful of current and former players when I hear them in commentary, see them on TV or notice that they are forging a successful public-speaking career, but I now realise and accept that, if women like me had not started to clear the way, to chart the new map, then they could not have followed. And this movement for more female leaders in this world is great – be that media work or public speaking or whatever else it may be. It is entirely the reason that I set up Inspiring Women: to provide a platform for more female voices, putting the female voice first.

More recently, when I deliver a speech at a new venue, to a rugby club that has never previously invited a woman speaker to their dinner, to a business, to a school, I feel a great and welcome responsibility. When I was the first ever female MC at Twickenham I enjoyed the responsibility,

I relished the pressure of the weight on my shoulders. I wanted to do a good job for my own sake, of course, but I realised at that moment that overwhelmingly I wanted to do a good job so that they would book another woman in the future. At that moment I didn't mind being the worker ant that I referred to in the first chapter and which I initially feared being. I love media work, but as I grow older I am forcing myself to be happy in the knowledge that I have helped to lay the foundations rather than reap the direct rewards myself. It doesn't by any means reduce the pain of not winning a World Cup but it certainly helps me to make peace with my own turmoil of emotions. And most importantly this understanding is helping me to once again look forward and not to cling to the past. There will always be battles to fight but now, if I let myself, I can enjoy watching them from afar rather than wishing I was in the middle. I still can't help resenting success in others but conversely alongside this I have an overwhelming desire and passion to contribute to that success, to provide a platform for the female voice, to help others to achieve and to ensure that in the future there will be no need for a company called Inspiring Women. My success and that of others like me will ultimately be our downfall.

'Inspire, Believe, Achieve' is the tag line of Inspiring Women. Self-motivation or belief follows external inspiration. Achievement is the outcome of belief. Those who achieve in some way can then inspire others. This is the cycle that I feel strongly about contributing to, whether through TRT and FITR, through contributing to the ever-increasing awareness, acceptance and now enjoyment of women's sport, or through my company. I never considered myself a feminist and I am still hesitant to do so now; I am probably more of a subtle suffragette, though I feel strongly and passionately about helping to ensure that there is equality of opportunity. This is why I am more than happy to have named my company 'Inspiring Women' and to give a platform to female speakers. There are not enough of them out there for a number of reasons, so I, just a girl from Folkestone, am trying to redress the balance.

I am not going to bang the drum every second and I still value and appreciate the differences between men and women. I love it when my husband opens the car door for me and it is an absolute necessity that he removes any spiders so that I do not have to. He doesn't let me take the bins out and he will carry the shopping. He knows that I am perfectly capable, but he wants me to be looked after for a change. He feels that after all these years I deserve it, and I am not going to argue with that. However, it is also important to celebrate and promote stories of female success so that others can take inspiration from them. It is also extremely important to understand that we have a value equal to that of our male counterparts and that is something I have continually stressed throughout this book. After years of competing in a sport where that value is only recently starting to be recognised by the wider public, this has been hard. By reading this book you will have gained some insight into the constant battles and knock-downs that on their own may seem insignificant but that add up to being quite draining and potentially damaging.

I don't think that we will ever see the crowds at women's games that we do at men's games. There is a deep-rooted behavioural trend that we cannot replicate. People follow men's sport to be part of something bigger. Whether a fan is watching on television or in the stands or listening to the radio or reading the sports pages, when their team has won they feel that they have contributed. They have been part of that victory and their emotional attachment is strong. We don't yet have that in women's sport. We have a followership of pure sports fans, watching the skill on display. We also have a growing movement of people encouraging the development of women's sport, but there is not this same sense of being part of the team, of being part of the victory. It is also my opinion that individuals still have a role. Securing a large sponsorship deal of course needs to make business sense to the sponsor company, but there are still one or two individuals within companies who drive that decision on a more personal, emotional level; an individual who is part of that wider team, who feels that strong emotional attachment. An individual who is in charge of a large organisation and can sponsor *their* team – by which they tend to mean their men's team. How do we build this in women's sport? And if we can't build this emotional attachment of being part of a wider team, of contributing to the on-field success of a group of personally unknown athletes, then we have to develop the idea that to sponsor women's sport makes good business sense. And that might require front-end loaded funding from national governing bodies until the external sponsorship follows. Deferred gratification, I believe it is called.

I personally cannot believe the amount of money that is poured into football. It makes me, quite frankly, angry. Imagine if we siphoned off just 1 per cent of all football sponsorship money, imagine what an impact that could have on other sports. And while we are at it, imagine what impact another 1 per cent could have on some of our poorer communities, not just here in the UK but around the world. But that is another issue entirely and not one I want to get into here. I don't get football. I understand the off-side rule, I know the aim of the game, but I don't see the beauty in it and I really, really, really don't understand why we continue to worship these men to such a level when all they are doing is running around a grass pitch for ninety minutes, shouting at the referee and diving on the floor, attempting to be awarded penalties. The actions of these individuals seen by millions on our TV screens have a direct impact on kids running around on smaller pitches on Sunday mornings. How are volunteer coaches supposed to explain to their team members that it is not OK to shout at referees when the young players are just copying their heroes? I recognise the simplicity of football, the jumpers for goalposts aspect of the game, and that I do like, that anyone can play it anywhere – but that is all I like about it. Women's football seems to have less of the cringe-worthy 'theatrics' of men's football and for that reason is slightly more bearable, but I still don't watch it. I felt guilty for a while that I wasn't supporting the women's team. I am a woman – surely I should be! But I just don't like football. I am all for equality, so whether it is our national men's team or national women's team I won't watch it. Not even Gareth Southgate's Waistcoat Revolution of 2018 convinced me otherwise.

The business world has become much more familiar to me over the last year and a half since setting up my own small company. I have learned to understand that it really is all about the contacts and that networking is key to business development. During the first couple of years after setting up Inspiring Women I did not attend a women's-only network group. I actively stayed away because I did not want to get pigeonholed and perceived as a raving feminist. I enjoy the company of men and I am not frightened to be in a male-dominated environment; in fact it is more comfortable for me than a female-dominated one – walking into a room full of women scares me. But I do understand that not every woman feels as confident or comfortable in a largely male environment where they can feel patronised or struggle to get their point across. The facts are there, discrimination against women has been prevalent in business and it is not yet extinct. Whether it is conscious or unconscious, it is not acceptable and neither is it in sport.

Unconscious bias has been a bit of a buzzword in recent years, but what actually is it and is there any way we can change it? Unconscious bias happens when our brains make very quick decisions about people or situations; we make a judgement in such a small fragment of time but the basis for this has been overlaid for a long time by the culture that we live in, our background, our personal experiences and social stereotypes; layer upon layer upon layer of perceptions, interpretations, images, experiences embedded within us. Some experiments have shown that unconscious bias in the business world can have an impact upon recruitment, salaries, job offers and so on. An unconscious judgement made by one individual can have a huge impact on someone else's life. In rugby, conscious bias exists in bucketloads but so does unconscious bias and this is more difficult to crack.

Much more difficult. I now understand that as much as we push for equality in the sport, it will take time, because of the years and years of history that have gone before us – but there are years ahead also and perceptions really are starting to change. The four-year-old daughter of one of the players in the Old Elthamians women's rugby team proudly announced that when she grew up she would be a princess *and* a rugby player. I absolutely love that.

So I feel passionately that there should be increased equality between men's and women's sport, I feel passionately that women should be paid equally in business and have the same opportunities to progress should they choose to do so, but I don't believe that the bias of other people is always the culprit. I don't think that we can always blame something or someone external to ourselves. Things are never that simple; sometimes women just do not push themselves forward enough. Women will generally, it seems, not apply for a promotion or a new job unless they tick every single box required. Women will sometimes not participate in sport because we don't like the way it makes us look, or we struggle to find the confidence to join a new team even if it is all female. These are barriers that we place on ourselves, but by sharing stories of success, by positively encouraging one another, we can start to make a change. We can gain confidence from the experience of others to help us in our journeys.

While I was working for the RFU we were starting to introduce a simple contact game to secondary-school girls rather than non-contact tag rugby. This was a challenge: many of the teachers lacked the confidence to train their students and some of the girls were a little hesitant. Others could not wait to be able to play full-contact rugby. At one tournament I purposely put the non-contact tag rugby pitch adjacent to the contact pitch for the age group we were trying to engage in contact rugby. At the start of the day most students were playing tag rugby, but as the day wore on more and more of the kids from the non-contact tag rugby pitch moved over to the contact pitch. They could see what their peers were doing, they gained confidence from their experience and thought, I can do that too. The teachers also saw that the game we were introducing was not complicated. We just needed to show them. And this is why it is important to show more women's sport on TV, so that younger girls can watch and think to themselves, I can do that. In an age where more and more young people are leading increasingly sedentary lives sitting indoors playing computer games, where unhealthy food is more accessible and the circumferences of our population's waists are increasing, encouraging women's sport as well as men's sport is crucial. It becomes more than a commercial decision surely.

Over the last four years I have learned a lot about being a woman; I have come to accept that we are different to men and that is completely fine. We should celebrate our differences and utilise our natural strengths, but there are also things we are not so good at. We are not so good at putting our hands up, we are not so good at pushing ourselves and applying for promotions, we struggle with our confidence and sometimes I believe we neglect ourselves and our own personal development. This is why it is OK to run workshops specifically for women. This is why it is more than OK to have founded a company and named it Inspiring Women.

I feel strongly about being a woman, about celebrating and enjoying that fact. I feel passionate about celebrating strong women, and I will ardently fight for women to have equal opportunities to make choices as they work their way through life. So, while we are fighting for equal rights, while we support International Women's Day in March, if that is what we choose to do, it is important to remember that we are different. And more importantly we must remember that our difference is OK; and actually, our differences are hugely beneficial when it comes to effective teamwork. The best teams are diverse and in business terms it has now been proven that organisations with a higher level of gender diversity on their boards see better financial returns. Little step by little step we will see improvements, and actually if we look back in time we have made some fairly massive strides. It was not all that long ago that women were not allowed their name on mortgages let alone requesting equal presence at board tables.

International Women's Day is a slightly controversial day. I think it is good in that it allows us to celebrate and highlight stories of successful women, but it has evolved particularly in the Western world. It didn't emerge because of gender pay-gap arguments or concerns over a glass ceiling; it emerged through various battles and fights for justice throughout North America and Europe, and it was the actions of women in Russia protesting against the backdrop of war in 1917 that led to the set date of 8 March each year. In 1975 it became a UN-recognised day and has since spread throughout the world. I do think that the founders, those who fought, risking their lives in the early days, would turn in their graves if they knew that for some organisations it is used simply to tick a gender diversity box once a year and then put it to bed for the remining 364 days of the year. But things are starting to change. CEOs, company directors and high-end decision-makers have spoken to me directly about their worries that they will lose talent and miss out on the recruitment of quality candidates if their gender diversity is not addressed. It is no longer that thing we talk about once a year; it is now seen as something that needs to be addressed with more than mere words. There are also complaints that there is no International Men's Day. There actually is one. The date is 19 November. It just does not have the same profile and following as International Women's day.

But I say again, it is also more than OK to be a woman. We don't have to be the same as men and that is exactly what diversity is: bringing different types of people together. That is what rugby has been for me and what many sports are for other people. In order to have the best teams it is vital that they are diverse. In rugby, particularly, if everyone had the same physicality or the same mentality, the team would fail. It is important to celebrate our differences and to understand how those differences contribute to high performance. But even if we are not involved in an environment concerned with high performance we can still celebrate ourselves as who we are. We can still be comfortable that, regardless of who we are, we can choose. Regardless of our gender we should not have to fight more battles in order to access the same opportunities. By writing this book, by using my influence in the rugby world, by setting up Inspiring Women, I am hoping to help others avoid the slammed doors that I have experienced. And one day, not only will we see greater diversity, but we will see true inclusion alongside this. We will not be present simply to tick boxes and to make up numbers but we will truly be present. Athletes or businesswomen or volunteers at club or county level, we will be present and influential; we just happen to be female.

Writing *Mud, Maul, Mascara* has been a form of therapy for me. During the few years involved in making this project come true, my thoughts, beliefs and emotions have started to settle. My bitterness, anger and resentment have started to subside. My husband has helped me to look forward. Walking down the aisle on 29 December 2017 represented so much for me. Of course, I could not wait to agree to spend the rest of my life with the man I love, but it also allowed me to start letting go. To look to the future. This book has enabled me to package up my conflicting emotions in these pages and tidy it up. To bring all of the loose ends together and help me to understand what is important. And to look forward more, to look back less. To be proud of my achievements and not resentful of my failures.

And what of the rose? We aspire to wear it on our shirt, then we become servants to it. The rose takes our energy, our lives. And then we leave the rose to someone else and we try to shape the rest of our life without it. The rose grows stronger with every new person who wears it and as it grows stronger it requires less from those who wear it. It drains less emotion and leaves less heartache. I leave the rose stronger in some ways, but this has taken its toll. It has taken me a while to recharge but I am getting there. And to heal my heart properly I finally need to allow myself that time to grieve; I need to give myself a break. It is a relationship that is not good for me, and that has taken too much from me. It has been one-sided. I want to become a rugby fan again and it will take time away from the game to build this back up.

As I reach the end of this book my dreams are starting to become more realistic. Not my dream of winning a World Cup – that, of course, will never come true – but my dreams of looking out of the kitchen window and watching my husband chop wood whilst our child is running around splashing in puddles in their wellies. At the time of writing this last paragraph I am nearly three months pregnant. The last three months have not been a joy; I am not 'glowing', by any stretch of the imagination; I have been grumpy, tired and feeling very sick morning, noon and night. Trying to get on with everyday life without friends or work associates figuring out what is going on has been a challenge. I am one week away from the all-important twelve-week scan, and all being well at the scan it will be a relief to share our news. As I have started to make strides and decisions in my working life, suddenly this development is posing further questions. It looks as though Jeremy and I will not be buying that convertible we craved, we will not be going on ten holidays a year and we will not be going away for weekend breaks on a last-minute whim. Hopefully, we will still be living life to the full, but we will have someone else to think about and share our life with. What does this mean for me, personally?

It means that I cannot help but look forward. Rugby may feature in our lives, I may be standing on the side of a mini rugby pitch on Sunday mornings in years to come, but I also may not be, and either is OK. As long as my child does not play football or Sevens I will be fine with whatever they do! They can even have a go at ballet, and will almost certainly be better at it than I ever was.

Whether our child is a girl or boy or both (twins would be daunting but great), my hope is that equality of opportunity is the norm as they grow up. I also hope that they are happy and comfortable with who they are. If they look up, they look around and they look forward, then I will be a proud mum. And would I want them to play rugby for England? In all honesty I don't think I would. I would love them to be involved in the game at a level where values are at the fore, but I don't think that this is true at the top level any more. I also would not want them to go through the emotional struggles that I have. But if it is the path that they choose to take I will be there for them. I may not get up at 5 a.m. on a Saturday to provide a taxi service as my dad did (I will never like early mornings) – that can be my husband's job – but I will support their choice. And choice really is what this book is all about, ensuring that there are opportunities to choose, whoever you are, wherever you are from, but also making sure that you are in control of your own choices. I lost control at different stages in my career and made choices that were not necessarily the right ones and have had to live with them ever since, but I have now started to make sense of them.

The next Women's World Cup is in 2021 and that is where my own World Cup story will end. It is time for new players, for new commentators, for new ambassadors and for new fans. The rose will continue to grow and I will be happy to observe from afar. I will still get excited by the perfect driving maul, I will enjoy fond memories of running around in the wet and mud in proper rugby-playing conditions, and as I put on my mascara I will be confident in the knowledge that a new breed of female rugby player is emerging: those that dream of being a princess and of playing rugby. My work here is done.

Acknowledgements

I would like to thank Katy Guest for offering me words of advice, encouragement and the all-important introduction to Unbound. I would like to thank Unbound for being different, for being innovative and giving more authors the opportunity to get their books published. To Ella Chappell: thank you for guiding me through the editing process.

To Stephen Jones once more: thank you for offering me advice, chatting through ideas in the early stages and giving me the confidence to continue. Thank you also for your long-time support of women's rugby.

Thank you to Folkestone Rugby Club; without you this book would never have been written, because this story never would have started. Angela Smith, your efforts to start our ladies' team, at a time when it was not the 'done thing', had so much of an impact upon me and my life. Thank you.

To my family: I am sure that there were parts of this book that you found hard to read and I am sorry for that. I hope that there were also parts that brought back some happy memories. Never a Christmas dinner goes by without any rugby chat. We are a rugby family; long may that continue.

Thank you again also to Jeremy, my husband and now also a great father to our beautiful little girl Mae Lois

Paynter, who was born on 21 May 2019. And Mae is where I will leave this with my last acknowledgement. Thank you, Mae, for your existence, for providing the perfect ending to this book. I wonder what your story will be?

Unbound is the world's first crowdfunding publisher, established in 2011.

We believe that wonderful things can happen when you clear a path for people who share a passion. That's why we've built a platform that brings together readers and authors to crowdfund books they believe in – and give fresh ideas that don't fit the traditional mould the chance they deserve.

This book is in your hands because readers made it possible. Everyone who pledged their support is listed below. Join them by visiting unbound.com and supporting a book today.

Paul Allen
Karen Allnutt
Ellie Ambridge
Millie Attwell
Neill Austin
Katherine Avery
Michael Aylwin
Peter Baggetta
Bruce Baker
Rebecca Bassenger
Glynis & Tom Beazley
Ali Bell
Phillip Bennett-Richards
Leslie Berry
Daniel Bettice

Will Biltcliffe
Daniel Birch
Andrew Black
Sam Brackley
Bev Bratton
Samantha Briggs
Janice Brown
Brian Browne
Caroline Burt
Stephen Butcher
Kelsi Butler
Ian Byers
Andy Carroll
Ian Carter
Rebecca Chanter

Anne-Laure Chappat
Ric Clark
David Clent
Simon Cloke
Gregory Collins
Luke Collins
Vicky Collins
Les Cooper
Natalie Cooper
Sammy Cooper
Ruth Cordero Peters
Claire Council
Joanne Courtenay
Jo Cox
Michael Crawley
Lottie Curling
Lorraine Dagger
Lesley Dampney
Ruth Daniels
Sean Davey
Julie Davies
Alice Davis
Sarah Davis
Darren Dawson
Sue Day
Jo Dobson (Baby Dobbo)
Steve Dobson (Dobbo)
Les Dodd
Patrick Dominey
Carrie Dunn
Nige Eccles
Claire Edginton
James Eldershaw
John Ellicock
Annekatrin Els

Stephen Ericson
Alys Evans
Claire Julia Feleppa
Trudie Fell
Claire Fergusson
Karen Fletcher
Rosie Foley
Danielle French
Victoria Frost
Lydia Furse
Sue Gardner
Nikki Gdn
C. Geng
Naomi Gibson
Andy Goater
Geoff Goodall
Paul J Goodison
Sarah Gough
Hannah Grant
Kristianne Gray
Adam Grindley
Ben Guest
Jonathan Guest
Katy Guest
John Paul Haden
Michelle Harvey
Beth Hawke
Wayne Hawley
Gareth Healy
Sophie Hemming
Paul Hengeveld
Ann Hepper
Charmian Heys
The Higby Family
Emily Hodder

Barbara Hodgkinson

Nick Hodsman

Anne Holland

Andrew Holloway

Leah Horan

CarrieAnne Horlock

Amanda Howland

Philip and Tricia Hutchinson

Inspiring Women

Rivka Isaacson

Johari Ismail

Bill James

Hilary Jeanes

Chris Jeffery

Nick Jenkins

Lara Jephson

Ian Jewkes

Sarah Johnson

Peter Joyner

Matt Kemp

Madeleine Kendall-Smith

Rhiannon Kennedy

Dan Kieran

Pierre L'Allier

Ewan Lawrie

Carol Lishman

Bridget Lumb

Faye Lygo

Catherine Makin

Marama

Victoria Mather

John 'Max' Maxwell

Tim May

Lucy McCappin

David McGuigan

Riëtte Meijer

Max & Clair Melville-Brown

Andrew Midgley

Katy Miller

Trevor Minter

Matt Mitchell

John Mitchinson

Suzanna Moggridge

Sinead Mullins

Rachel Murphy

Carlo Navato

Cindy Nelles

John New

Danielle Nichols

Mark O'Neill

Georgia Odd

John Osborn

Ospreys U18 Women, Ottawa, Canada

Sally Parker

Alex Paske

Kobus Paulsen

Jeremy Paynter

Bruce Perkins

Jackie Perkins

Claire Phillips

Elizabeth Philp

Justin Pollard

Jennie Powell

Jo Proctor

Dave Ramsbottom

Angharad Reakes

Mike Reakes

Karen Roberts

Andrew Robinson

Supporters

Justine Robinson
David Rose
Sophy Roseaman
Lucy Ross-Mackenzie
Nicole Rowland
Alex Ruddock
Martin Russell
Emily Ryall
Christian Sangiuseppe
Daniel Sangiuseppe
Tanja Schmitz
Paul Schofield
Elly Scott
Corrie Shackle
Bethan Shaw
Ang Sheppard
Shepway Sports Trust
Sarah Shipley
Andrew Shurmer
Caroline Shutter
Lisa Sleep
May Sly
Hannah Smith
Ian Smith
Ivor Smith
Kate Smith
Katie Smith
Marc Smith
Matthew Smith
Nicky Smith
Nigel Smith
Paddy Smith
Joseph Somerville
Sarah Souter
Gregory Spencer

Helen Spencer
Ivor Spencer
Martin Spencer
Nigel and Jane Spencer
Rosie Spiegelhalter
Richard Stone
Paul Sugars
Bethan Taylor
Richard Taylor
Beth & Hannah Thomas
Trish Thurley
Jon Tickle
Kezza TownRatt
Stuart Tracey
Sarah Trigg
Maia Tua-Davidson
Jenny and Phil Tuckwell
Jon Turbutt
Don & Yvonne Turner
John Turner
Elizabeth Vallance
Vidal-Nel family
Lucy Vidler
Melissa Wallis
Clare Walsh
Bina Walti
Sascha Walti
Urs Walti
Zara Walton
Diane and Alfie Ward
    and Cashmore
Juliette Warren
Paul Watson
Angela Weir
Pamela Welsh

Sam West
Katherine Wijnsma
Nancy Wilkinson
Helen Williams
Anna Willson
Jo Wimble-Groves
Lucinda Winter
The Women's Rugby Show
Paul Wood

Wooden Spoon
Michelle Woodger
Darren Woods
Stuart Woollford
Kate Worlock
Wren children of Clevedon:
    Rosie, Tabs & Jim
Zoological Society of London